Written by
Kathy Howell and Alisa Webb

Editor: Kim Cernek

Illustrator: Darcy Tom

Cover Photographer: Michael Jarrett

Cover Illustrator: Kimberlee Graves

Designer: Corina Chien

Cover Designer: Corina Chien

Art Director: Tom Cochrane

Project Director: Carolea Williams

Table of Contents

Introduction

No child can resist the charm of a wrapped gift. Colorful paper and shiny bows grab children's attention and suggest that something equally as interesting is inside. *Literacy Bags* gives you dozens of ways to organize 26 thematic mini-units from A–Z in fabulous "packages" that children cannot wait to handle!

This resource presents each letter of the alphabet as a mini-unit designed to give children practice with fundamental skills. Developmentally appropriate games and activities, as well as books, props, snacks, and other items that relate to the theme, are stored in one of several inviting bags or containers that you create from simple, easy-to-find items and personalize with art supplies. These customized containers not only fascinate children but also provide you with an easy way to manage your materials and send them home for children to share with their families.

Detailed materials lists, clear activity directions, instruction cards for completing the activities, templates for making student and parent journals, lists of literature links, and a parent letter that introduces the *Literacy Bags* program are included in this book. Use these tools to create versatile, valuable lessons that give children opportunities to practice several language, math, science, social studies, writing, and thinking skills. Or, add your own activities to the bags to supplement your district and state curriculum objectives.

Once you have collected and prepared the materials for a mini-unit and placed them in the customized kit, children will have no difficulty participating in the games and activities independently or with a small group at a center. And, these marvelous mini-units travel very well. Send home the kits to strengthen your home–school connection and give children a chance to practice their skills, parents an idea of what their child is learning in your class, and families another opportunity to spend quality time together.

Pack your bags and get ready to learn. It's as easy as A-B-C!

Getting Started

Imagine It: Creating a Kit

Choose a mini-unit, and follow the simple directions to create a thematic kit, or use the suggestions below to make a kit from a different type of container. Keep in mind that the kit should be durable and manageable because it will change hands many times over the course of the year.

Fabric Bags

Choose a fabric with a print that coordinates with your theme. Drapery fabrics, polished cottons, and denims provide the sturdiness necessary for holding unit items. 100% cotton fabrics can also be used but should be doubled for support.

Cut two 20" x 14" (51 cm x 36 cm) rectangles from the fabric. Place them back-to-back so that the front sides of the patterns touch. (At this stage, the unsewn bag looks as if it is inside out.) Use a needle and thread or a sewing machine to stitch together the sides and bottom of the bag. Cut two 16" (40.5 cm) strips, and sew the ends of each strip to the top of the bag to create two handles. Turn the fabric inside out so that the front side of the fabric shows. As an option, cut out a square from the same fabric or a coordinating fabric, and sew it on the bag to create a pocket.

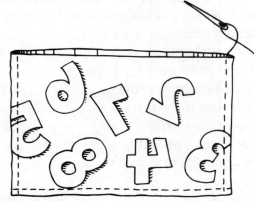 

Other Containers

Get the word out that you are searching for fun containers for your mini-units. You never know what a parent, friend, neighbor, or relative may have stored away in his or her basement or attic. Collect containers such as these:

- backpack
- duffel bag
- lunch box
- beach bag
- bucket
- divided make-up box
- gift bag
- toolbox

- pillowcase
- tackle box
- detergent box
- suitcase
- overnight bag
- large purse
- large pail or bucket

Make It: Preparing the Materials

Each unit outlines ideas for preparing each kit. Choose from the suggestions what you would like to include in your kits. Each mini-unit should be tailored to the needs of your class and the materials that are available to you. The following suggestions will likely spark your ideas about what to place in your kits.

Literature Links

Collect various books that relate to the theme of the mini-unit or specific lessons in the mini-unit, and place a few in the kit for children to share with each other and their families.

Props

Add to the kit factory-made and homemade toys, stuffed animals, and puppets that relate to the letter or theme of the mini-unit. Encourage children to use these props to retell stories or make up their own.

Snacks

Each mini-unit features suggestions for snacks that coordinate with the theme or games and activities. Encourage children to use these food items for sorting, sharing, graphing, dividing, and identifying initial sounds. Adding food to a kit is a fun little extra touch, but it is an optional part of the program.

Journals

Include a student journal and a parent journal in each kit. These journals give children and parents an opportunity to respond to the games and activities they have explored. To make a journal, copy the journal reproducible for the mini-unit on card stock, cut apart the paper along the dotted line, and laminate both pieces. These pieces will serve as the front covers of the student and parent journals. Laminate another blank piece of card stock, and cut it in half to make the back covers for the journals. Cut 10–20 pieces of white copy paper in half. Place a stack of paper between each laminated cover, and hole-punch two holes at the top. Insert a metal ring in each hole, and place the journals in the kit. Make one student journal and one parent journal for each mini-unit. Refill the white copy paper as needed.

Games and Activities

For each mini-unit, read the Preparations section, and decide what you want to include in the kit. This section describes the materials you need to collect, prepare, and place in the kit.

Instruction Cards

Each game and activity comes with a coordinating instruction card that features directions written directly to the children. Copy the cards on card stock, laminate them, cut them apart, and attach them to their corresponding game or activity. Create new cards for games or activities that you develop on your own, and add them to the kit.

Reproducibles

Make the necessary copies of the reproducibles that correspond with the games and activities, and place them in the kit.

Inventory List

Record the contents of each kit on the Inventory List (page 8). Copy the reproducible, and write the title of the mini-unit on the top line. List below the books, props, snacks, games, activities, and other materials you have included in the kit. Laminate the list, and either glue, tape, or pin it directly to the kit. Or, hole-punch the paper, and use a piece of ribbon or string to tie it to the outside of the kit. As an option, tape a copy of your class list to the back of the inventory list. Encourage children to cross off their name after they have shared the kit with their family.

Checkout Chart

Make a simple checkout chart to track the kits and ensure that children have taken each one home. Copy the Checkout Chart (page 9) on card stock, and laminate it. Use a transparency marker to write the name of each child in class in the first column. When a child takes home a kit, use a green transparency marker to draw a checkmark beside his or her name in the column for the kit. When the child returns the kit, erase the green checkmark, and use a red transparency marker to draw another checkmark.

Take It: Using the Materials

Once you have assembled the kits, make them available to your class for use in a variety of settings. When sending home the kits, encourage children to explore them for a few days and then return them intact for another child to investigate.

Center Work

Introduce the theme and contents of a kit to your class. Make sure that children understand how to complete each game and activity. Then, make the kit available to children for use during center time.

I'm Done!

Invite children who finish their work early to read one of the books or complete one of the games or activities in a kit.

Volunteers

Invite parents or older students in your school to visit your class and explore the contents of a kit with a group of children.

Home and Back

Encourage children to take home a kit for a few days. Use the Checkout Chart (page 9) to determine who has checked out each kit.

Tips

- Stock up on large and small resealable bags, file folders, card stock, transparency markers, crayons, markers, colored pencils, and tape. These materials are used in a majority of the games and activities.
- To make the resealable bags more manageable, cut small slits in the bottom to let air escape. Always write on the outside of the kit detailed descriptions of the contents in the bags. Staple small bags to the file folders or games to which they belong.
- Label everything that goes into a kit with your school name and grade level.
- Remember that some materials (e.g., snacks) may need to be replaced from time to time.
- Check the kits periodically to determine whether additional copies of reproducibles are needed.
- Store kits in large plastic tubs or on hooks when they are not in circulation.
- Keep a large box filled with extra materials, including reproducibles, journal materials, resealable bags, and other things that might need to be replaced over the course of the year. You might consider making an additional set of the games and activities that involve small pieces in the event that some are lost. Keep extra snack items in a separate box.

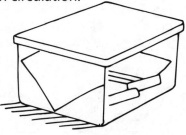

Inventory List

Please find the following items in this kit titled

_____.

1. _____

2. _____

3. _____

4. _____

5. _____

6. _____

7. _____

8. _____

Checkout Chart

	Apple Activities	Back-to-Work Briefcase	Camping with Critters	Dinosaur Duffel Bag	Elephant's Everything Trunk	Fun with Friends and Family	Giraffe's Gym Bag	Happy Hearts Bag	Inchworm's Interesting Bag	Jammin' Jungle Bag	Kitchen Kit	Ladybug's Luggage	Making Magic	Number Fun Notebook	Our Outing to the Ocean	Packing for a Picnic	Queen's Quilt Bag	Reading Rodeo	Science Sack	Teddy Bear's Toolbox	Uncle Sam's U.S.A. Bag	Bon Voyage Vacation Bag	Waterworks	Our Exciting Box	A Year to Remember	Zigzag Bag
1.																										
2.																										
3.																										
4.																										
5.																										
6.																										
7.																										
8.																										
9.																										
10.																										
11.																										
12.																										
13.																										
14.																										
15.																										
16.																										
17.																										
18.																										
19.																										
20.																										
21.																										
22.																										
23.																										
24.																										
25.																										

Parent Letter

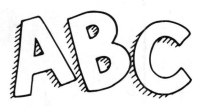

Dear Parents,

An important part of your child's primary school experience is to develop prereading skills, one of which is learning the letters and sounds of the alphabet. During the course of the year, your child will bring home a series of alphabet kits that contain developmentally appropriate games and activities, as well as books, props, snacks, and other items that reinforce prereading skills. Use these tools to help your child practice language skills, as well as a variety of math, science, social studies, writing, and critical thinking skills.

Your child has worked with the kits in the classroom. The kits are designed for you to use with ease at home and include materials and instruction cards for completing all the games and activities. You will also find student journals for your child to use to reflect upon his or her work and parent journals you can use to communicate your comments and questions to me. These kits can also be considered as assessment tools because they will help you identify firsthand the skills your child has mastered and those he or she needs to continue practicing.

When your child brings home a kit, feel free to take a few days to explore its contents with him or her. When your child is ready to return a kit, please ensure that each item on the inventory list is in the kit.

The children enjoy these fun and inviting kits in part because of the interesting contents but mostly because they are able to share the joy of learning to read with you!

Thanks,

Apple Activities

Find a large basket, and paint several apples on the sides of it. Or, cut out apples from craft foam, felt, or fabric, and use hot glue or fabric glue to attach them to the basket. Paint *Apple Activities* on the side of the basket.

Alternative Theme Ideas

- Find fabric with an airplane, alligator, alphabet, animal, ant, apple, or astronaut print, and use it to make a bag (see page 4).

- Use a purse or carrying case made from imitation alligator hide.

Literature Links

- *Animals Should Definitely Not Wear Clothing* by Judi Barrett (Aladdin)
- *An Anteater Named Arthur* by Bernard Waber (Houghton Mifflin)
- *Apron Annie in the Garden* by Joellyn Cicciarelli (Creative Teaching Press)
- *Eating the Alphabet* by Lois Ehlert (Harcourt)
- *For Pete's Sake* by Ellen Stoll Walsh (Harcourt)

- *I Can't Said the Ant* by Polly Cameron (Scholastic)
- *I Want to Be an Astronaut* by Byron Barton (HarperFestival)
- *The Lady with the Alligator Purse* by Nadine Bernard Westcott (Little, Brown and Company)
- *The Seasons of Arnold's Apple Tree* by Gail Gibbons (Harcourt)
- *Very Boring Alligator* by Jean Gralley (Henry Holt and Company)

Playtime Props

★ alligator or ant stuffed animals or puppets

★ astronaut figure

★ foam or magnetic letters

★ plastic or wooden apples

★ toy airplane or ambulance

Snacks to Sort, Sound Out, and Share

♥ animal crackers

♥ dried apples or apple fruit snacks

♥ Famous Amos® mini-cookies

♥ raisins for "ants"

Apple Activities
Parent Journal

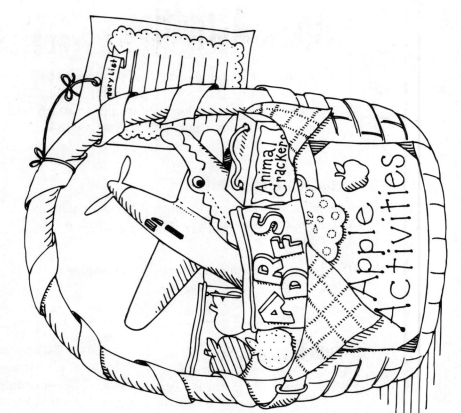

Please use this journal to record your comments or questions about the games and activities you have enjoyed with your child.

Apple Activities
Student Journal

Here are some of the things you can write in this journal.

1. Read one of the books in the kit, and write about your favorite part of the story.

2. Write your own story.

3. Write about something that you have eaten that was made with apples.

4. List as many words as you can that begin with the letter *a*.

5. Write about your favorite game or activity in this kit. Tell why you liked it.

Remember: Always write your name before you write anything else in the journal!

Apple Activities Preparations

Apple Words

| Children will practice reading high-frequency words that begin with the letter *a*. |

Make two copies of the **Apples reproducible (page 15)** on **red card stock**, and cut out the twelve apples. Write one of the following high-frequency words on each apple: *about, all, along, also, am, an, and, any, are, as, asked*, and *at*. Put the apple cutouts and the **Apple Words instruction card (page 14)** in a **resealable bag**, and place the bag in the kit.

Apple Tree ABC

| Children will use alphabetical order to connect dots to make a picture. |

Copy the **Apple Tree ABC reproducible (page 16)**, and laminate it. Tie a **string** to one end of a **transparency marker**. Hole-punch the top of the reproducible, and tie the other end of the string through it. Put the paper and the **Apple Tree ABC instruction card (page 14)** in a **resealable bag**, and place the bag in the kit.

Apple Graph

| Children will sort apple cutouts by color and graph the data. |

Make two copies of the **Apples reproducible (page 15)**, cut out the apples, and color ten of the apples to make three green apples, four red apples, and three yellow apples. Laminate the apple cutouts, and put them in a **resealable bag**. Copy the **Graph reproducible (page 17)**. Open a **file folder**, and glue the paper to the right side. On the left side, write *1. Which color has the most? 2. Which colors have the same amount? 3. How many apples are there in all?* Glue the **Apple Graph instruction card (page 14)** and the two remaining apples to the front of the folder, and laminate it. Place the folder and the bag in the kit.

Apple Activities Instruction Cards

Materials

- red apple cutouts
- student journal

Apple Words

1. Place the apple cutouts facedown in a pile.
2. Turn over a cutout, and try to read the word on it. If you can read the word, keep it. If you cannot read the word, return it to the bottom of the pile.
3. Keep turning over cutouts until you can read all twelve words.
4. Write the words in the student journal.
5. Place all the apple cutouts back in the bag, and return all items to the kit.

Materials

- Apple Tree ABC paper
- transparency marker
- paper towel

Apple Tree ABC

1. Use the special marker to connect the dots in ABC order. Begin with the letter *A* and end with the letter *Z*.
2. When you are done, use a damp paper towel to wipe away the picture.
3. Return all items to the kit.

Materials

- Apple Graph folder
- red, green, and yellow apple cutouts
- student journal

Apple Graph

1. Open the folder, and place it on a flat surface.
2. Arrange the apple cutouts on the graph.
3. Write the answers to the questions in the student journal.
4. Place the apple cutouts back in the bag, and return all items to the kit.

Apples

Apple Tree ABC

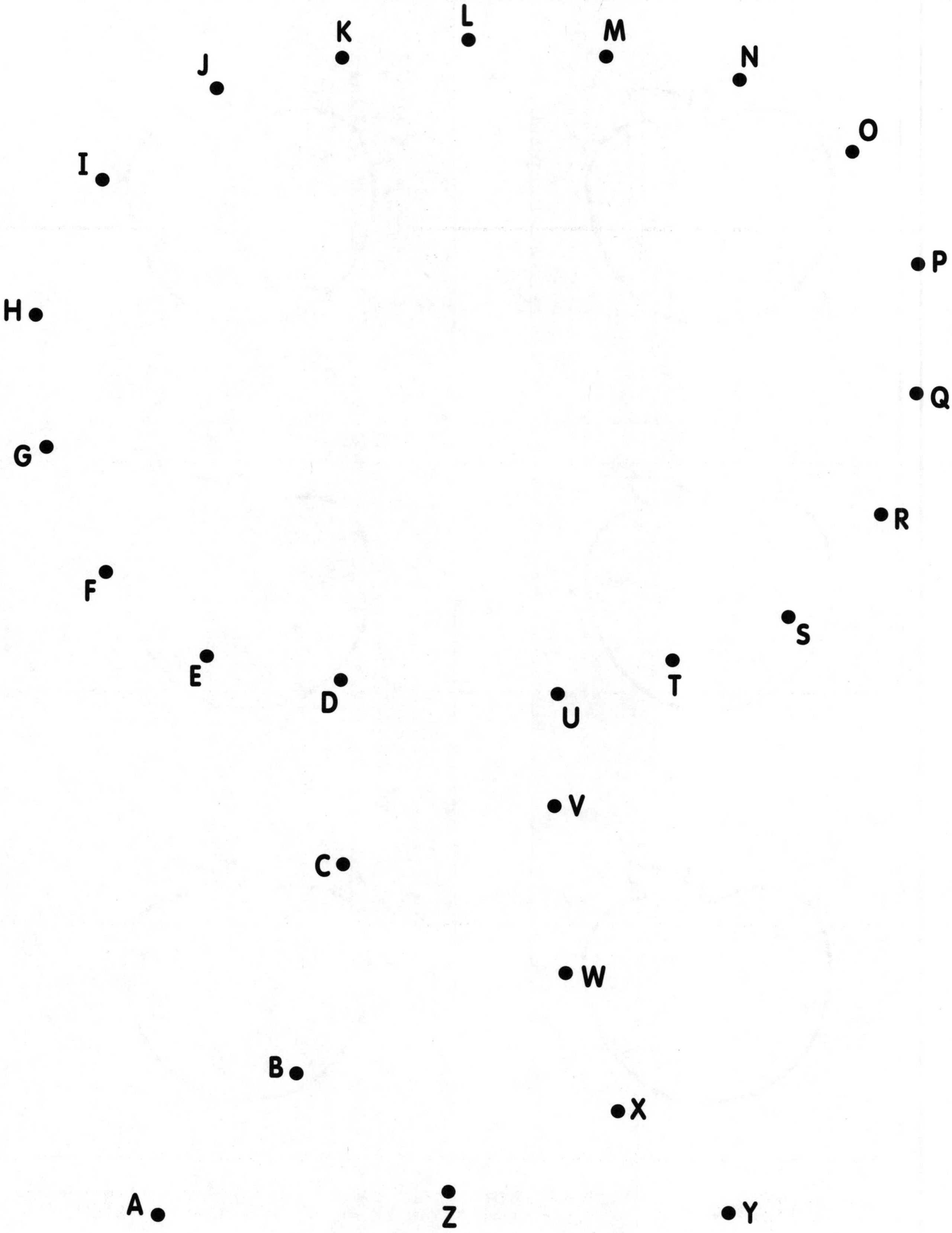

J •   K •   L •   M •   N •

O •

I •

P •

H •

Q •

G •

R •

F •

S •

E •

T •

D •

U •

V •

C •

W •

B •

X •

A •   Z •   Y •

Graph

| red apples | green apples | yellow apples |

Back-to-Work Briefcase

Find a large briefcase. Use a paint marker to write *Back-to-Work Briefcase* on the side of it.

Alternative Theme Ideas

- Find fabric with a baby, bear, bee, bug, or bunny print, and use it to make a bag (see page 4).

- Use a paint marker to write *Back-to-Work Backpack* on one side of a backpack.

Literature Links

- → *The Baby Bears* by Sonja Bullaty and Angelo Lomeo (Golden Press)
- → *The Berenstain's B Book* by Stan Berenstain (Random House)
- → *Brown Bear, Brown Bear What Do You See?* by Bill Martin Jr. and Eric Carle (Henry Holt and Company)
- → *Bunny Cakes* by Rosemary Wells (Dial Books)

- → *Buttons, Buttons* by Rozanne Lanczak Williams (Creative Teaching Press)
- → *Jimmy's Boa* by Trinka Hakes Noble (Dial Books)
- → *Let's Go Home Little Bear* by Martin Waddell (Candlewick Press)
- → *Little Bear* by Else Holmelund Minarik (HarperTrophy)
- → *Read to Your Bunny* by Rosemary Wells (Scholastic)
- → *The Runaway Bunny* by Margaret Wise Brown (HarperCollins)

Playtime Props

★ baby, bear, bee, bug, or bunny stuffed animals or puppets

★ balls

★ bingo game

★ binoculars

★ Boggle, Jr. ®

★ bubbles

★ bunny-ear headband

★ business supplies (e.g., stamp pad, date stamper, sticky notes)

★ plastic or wooden boat

Snacks to Sort, Sound Out, and Share

♥ bubble gum

♥ butter cookies

♥ mini-bagels

♥ Teddy Grahams® crackers

Back-to-Work Briefcase
Student Journal

Here are some of the things you can write in this journal.

1. Read one of the books in the kit, and write about your favorite part of the story.

2. Write your own story.

3. Write about a job you might like to have some-day.

4. List as many words as you can that begin with the letter b.

5. Write about your favorite game or activity in this kit. Tell why you liked it.

Remember: Always write your name before you write anything else in the journal!

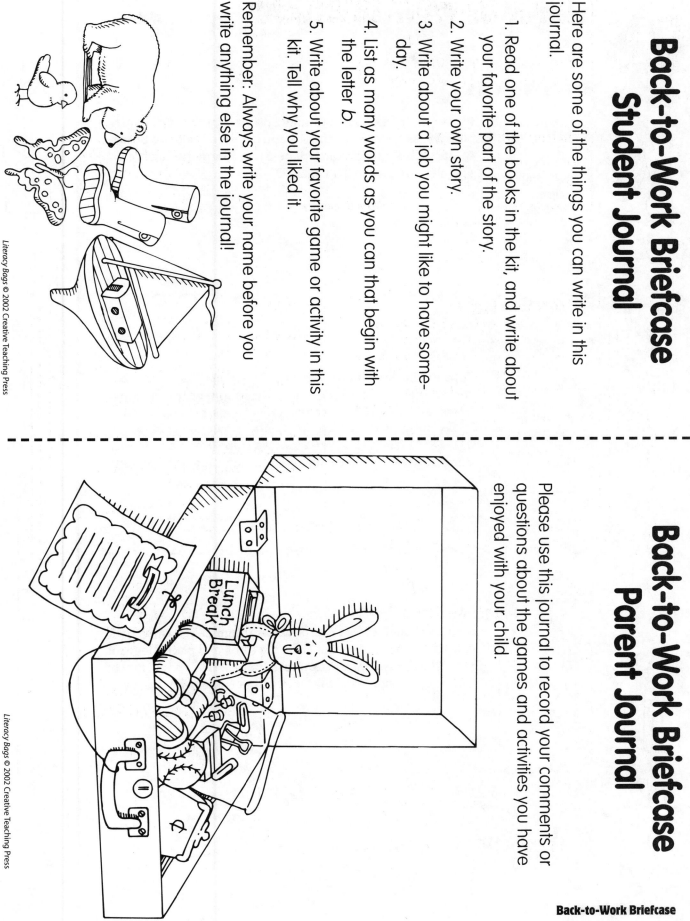

Back-to-Work Briefcase
Parent Journal

Please use this journal to record your comments or questions about the games and activities you have enjoyed with your child.

Back-to-Work Briefcase Preparations

Boss's Briefcase

Children will sort objects by type.

Place a **divided plastic container**, **office supplies (e.g., paper clips, brass fasteners, rubber bands, erasers)**, and the **Boss's Briefcase instruction card (page 21)** in a **large resealable bag**, and place the bag in the kit.

Business Cents

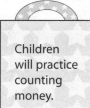

Children will practice counting money.

Copy the **Business Cents reproducible (page 22)** on **colored card stock**, and laminate it. Place **office supplies (paper clips, brass fasteners, rubber bands, small labels, erasers, small sticky notes)** and the **Business Cents instruction card (page 21)** in a **resealable bag**. Put **assorted coins (pennies, nickels, dimes, quarters)** in a **change purse or small resealable bag**. Place all items in the kit.

Lunch Break!

Children will sort picture cards by beginning sounds.

Copy the **Lunch Break! reproducible (page 23)** on **card stock**, color it, and laminate it. Cut apart the cards, and place them and the **Lunch Break! instruction card (page 21)** in a **small lunch box or container**. Place the lunch box or container in the kit.

Back-to-Work Briefcase Instruction Cards

Materials
- office supplies
- divided container

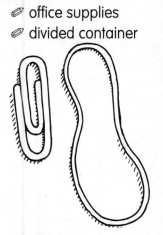

Boss's Briefcase

1. Sort the objects by type into the sections of the container.
2. Return all items to the kit.

Materials
- Business Cents paper
- office supplies
- coins

Business Cents

1. Pick an object, and look at the paper to see how much it costs.
2. Place the correct coins beside the matching picture on the paper.
3. Place the supplies and coins back in the bags, and return all items to the kit.

Materials
- lunch box or container of cards
- student journal

Lunch Break!

1. Remove the cards from the lunch box or container.
2. Place only the cards with foods that begin with the letter *b* back into the lunch box or container.
3. Think of other foods that begin with the letter *b*, and write them in the student journal.
4. Place all the cards back in the lunch box or container.
5. Return all items to the kit.

Business Cents

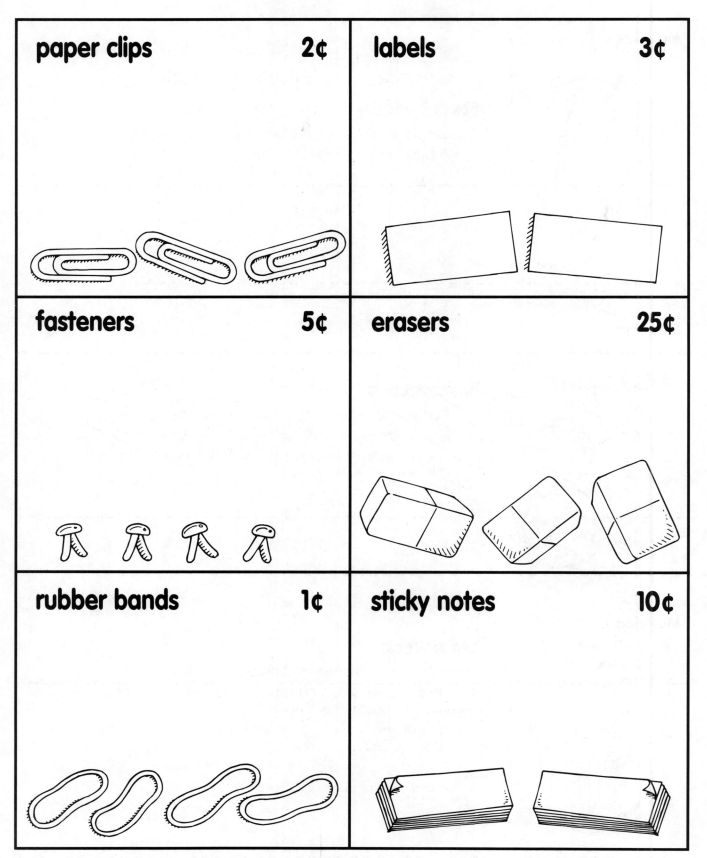

paper clips **2¢**	**labels** **3¢**
fasteners **5¢**	**erasers** **25¢**
rubber bands **1¢**	**sticky notes** **10¢**

Lunch Break!

banana

apple

bacon

milk

beans

butter

cookie

broccoli

bread

carrot

Camping with Critters

Use art supplies to write *Camping with Critters* on a backpack.

Alternative Theme Ideas

- Find corduroy or fabric with a cat, cookie, or cowhide print, and use it to make a bag (see page 4).

- Use a divided make-up case or a medium-sized nylon cooler or picnic bag.

Literature Links

- *Cat Up a Tree* by John Hassett (Houghton Mifflin)
- *Cat, What Is That?* by Tony Johnston (HarperCollins)
- *Chicka Chicka Boom Boom* by Bill Martin Jr. and John Archambault (Simon & Schuster)
- *Cookie's Week* by Cindy Ward (Scholastic)
- *The Crayola® Counting Book* by Rozanne Lanczak Williams (Creative Teaching Press)
- *Itchy, Itchy Chicken Pox* by Grace Maccarone (Scholastic)
- *Just Me and My Dad* by Mercer Mayer (Golden Book)
- *Mama Cat Has Three Kittens* by Denise Fleming (Henry Holt and Company)
- *The Very Hungry Caterpillar* by Eric Carle (Philomel)
- *Who Took the Cookies from the Cookie Jar?* by Bonnie Lass (Little, Brown and Company)

Playtime Props

★ calculator

★ camel, cat, caterpillar, chicken, or cow stuffed animals or puppets

★ Candyland®

★ card games

★ cassettes/cassette player with headphones

★ checkers

★ clock and/or telling time games

★ clown doll or figure

★ counting board games

★ plastic cookies

★ toy cars

Snacks to Sort, Sound Out, and Share

♥ candy corn

♥ Cheerios® cereal

♥ Cap'n Crunch® cereal

♥ Cracker Jacks®

♥ crackers

♥ Creme Savers®

Camping with Critters
Student Journal

Here are some of the things you can write in this journal.

1. Read one of the books in the kit, and write about your favorite part of the story.

2. Write your own story.

3. Write about a camping adventure you have had or one you would like to take.

4. List as many words as you can that begin with the letter c.

5. Write about your favorite game or activity in this kit. Tell why you liked it.

Remember: Always write your name before you write anything else in the journal!

Camping with Critters
Parent Journal

Please use this journal to record your comments or questions about the games and activities you have enjoyed with your child.

Camping with Critters Preparations

Camping Tools Clothespin Match

Children will identify the beginning sounds and letters of words.

Copy the **Camping Tools reproducible (page 28)** on **card stock**, and cut apart the cards. Laminate the cards, and place them in a **resealable bag**. Use a **permanent marker** to write the letters *b, c, f, h, l, m, n, p, r, s, t,* and *w* on separate **spring-loaded clothespins**, and place them and the **Camping Tools Clothespin Match instruction card (page 27)** in the resealable bag. Place the bag in the kit.

Shining a Light on Patterns

Children will use three items to make a pattern.

Copy the **Shining a Light on Patterns reproducible (page 29)** for each child, and place the copies in a **file folder**. Place a sheet of **construction paper** for each child in the same folder. Tape the **Shining a Light on Patterns instruction card (page 27)** to the cover of the folder, and place the folder in the kit.

Critter Capers

Children will write and illustrate a story.

Hole-punch a piece of **white paper** for each child, and put the papers in a **three-ring binder**. Tape the **Critter Capers instruction card (page 27)** to the front of the binder. Place the binder in the kit.

Camping with Critters Instruction Cards

Materials
- Camping Tools cards
- clothespins

Camping Tools Clothespin Match

1. Look at the picture on each card. Choose the clothespin that has the same beginning sound as the picture, and clip it to the card.
2. Place the cards and clothespins back in the bag.
3. Return all items to the kit.

Materials
- folder
- crayons or markers
- scissors
- glue/glue stick
- construction paper

Shining a Light on Patterns

1. Remove a paper from the folder, and decide what a flashlight, lantern, and campfire have in common.
2. Color and cut out the pictures, and use them to make different patterns.
3. Choose your favorite pattern, and glue it to a piece of construction paper.
4. Write your name on the paper, and place it in the folder.
5. Return all items to the kit.

Materials
- binder
- crayons or markers

Critter Capers

1. Open the binder, and carefully remove a blank page.
2. Think of a critter that begins with the letter c, such as a camel, a cat, a caterpillar, a cheetah, a cow, or a crow.
3. Draw a picture of you and the critter at the top of the paper.
4. Write a story about what you and the critter did while you were camping at the bottom of the paper.
5. Place your paper back in the binder.
6. Return all items to the kit.

Literacy Bags © 2002 Creative Teaching Press

Camping Tools

_ackpack

_leeping bag

_ent

_ampfire

_ap

_lashlight

_antern

_ot dog

_an

_ope

_et

_ater

Literacy Bags © 2002 Creative Teaching Press

Shining a Light on Patterns

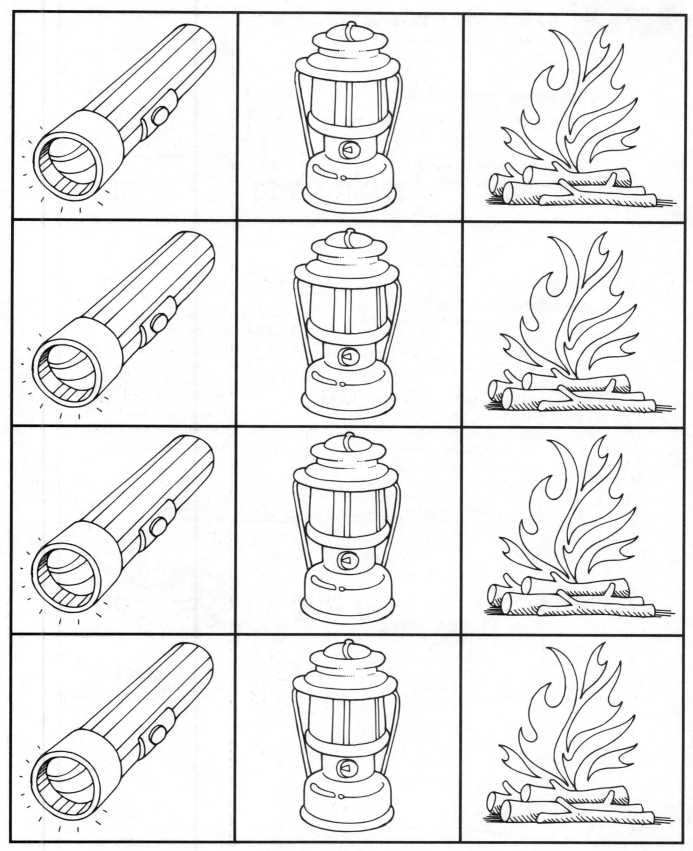

Dinosaur Duffel Bag

Use fabric markers to draw dinosaurs or dinosaur footprints on a duffel bag. Use a fabric marker to write *Dinosaur Duffel Bag* on one side.

Alternative Theme Ideas

- Find fabric with a dinosaur or dog print, and use it to make a bag (see page 4).

- Find fabric with a cow or barnyard print, and make a bag, or paint black spots on the outside of a pail for a dairy theme.

- Use a large doctor's bag.

Literature Links

- *ABC Dogs* by Kathy Darling (Walker & Company)
- *All Through the Week with Cat and Dog* by Rozanne Lanczak Williams (Creative Teaching Press)
- *Dinosaur Roar!* by Paul and Henrietta Stickland (Dutton)
- *Dinosaurs Dancing* by Luella Connelly (Creative Teaching Press)
- *Dinosaurs, Dinosaurs* by Byron Barton (Crowell)
- *Good Dog, Carl* by Alexandra Day (Simon & Schuster)
- *Harry the Dirty Dog* by Gene Zion (HarperCollins)
- *How Do Dinosaurs Say Goodnight?* by Jane Yolen (Scholastic)
- *If the Dinosaurs Came Back* by Bernard Most (Harcourt)
- *Patrick's Dinosaur* by Carol Carrick (Clarion Books)

Playtime Props

★ dalmatian, dinosaur, dog, or dragon stuffed animals or puppets

★ dentist's kit

★ dice games

★ doctor's kit

★ doll

★ dominoes

★ rubber duck

Snacks to Sort, Sound Out, and Share

♥ dates

♥ dinosaur fruit snacks

♥ Dum Dum® suckers

Dinosaur Duffel Bag
Student Journal

Here are some of the things you can write in this journal.

1. Read one of the books in the kit, and write about your favorite part of the story.

2. Write your own story.

3. Imagine that you find dinosaurs in your backyard, and write about what happens next.

4. List as many words as you can that begin with the letter *d*.

5. Write about your favorite game or activity in this kit. Tell why you liked it.

Remember: Always write your name before you write anything else in the journal!

Literacy Bags © 2002 Creative Teaching Press

Dinosaur Duffel Bag
Parent Journal

Please use this journal to record your comments or questions about the games and activities you have enjoyed with your child.

Literacy Bags © 2002 Creative Teaching Press

Dinosaur Duffel Bag Preparations

Dinosaur Sorting

Children will sort dinosaurs by color.

Fold a piece of **white paper** into fourths. Color each rectangle on the paper one of the colors of **dinosaur manipulatives (4 different colors)**, and laminate it. Put the dinosaur manipulatives and the **Dinosaur Sorting instruction card (page 33)** in a **resealable bag**, and place all items in the kit.

Dinosaur Dice

Children will practice writing simple addition equations.

Put **adding machine tape**, **dice**, and the **Dinosaur Dice instruction card (page 33)** in a **large resealable bag**, and place the bag in the kit.

Dinosaur Detective

Children will identify words that begin with the letter *d*.

Copy the **Dinosaur Detective reproducibles (pages 34–35)**, and color them. Open a **file folder**, and glue a reproducible to each side. Glue the **Dinosaur Detective instruction card (page 33)** to the cover of the folder, and laminate it. Clip a **transparency marker** to the folder, and place the folder in the kit.

Dinosaur Duffel Bag Instruction Cards

Materials

- multicolored sorting paper
- dinosaurs
- crayons or markers
- student journal

Dinosaur Sorting

1. Place the paper with the colored rectangles on a flat surface.
2. Sort the dinosaurs by color on the paper.
3. On the back of the paper, make a pattern with the dinosaurs.
4. Draw a picture of your pattern in the student journal.
5. Place the dinosaurs back in the bag, and return all items to the kit.

Materials

- adding machine tape
- dice

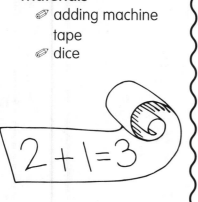

Dinosaur Dice

1. Tear off a strip of adding machine tape.
2. Roll the dice, and use the number on each die to write an addition sentence. For example, if you roll 2 and 3 you could write 2 + 3.
3. Count the number of dots on both dice to determine the sum or answer, and write it at the end of the equation (e.g., 2 + 3 = 5).
4. Roll the dice nine more times, and write an addition sentence for each set of numbers.
5. Return all items to the kit.

Materials

- folder
- transparency marker
- paper towel

Dinosaur Detective

1. Open the folder, and look at the pictures inside. Name each picture.
2. Use the special marker to write *d* below each picture that begins with *d*.
3. Ask someone to check your work.
4. Use a damp paper towel to wipe away your work.
5. Return all items to the kit.

Dinosaur Detective

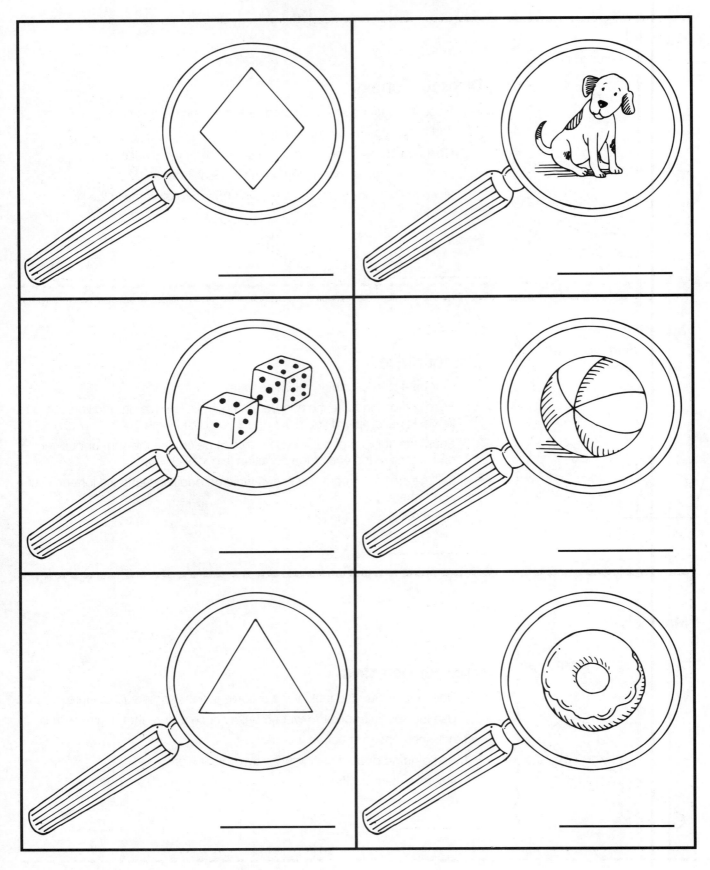

Dinosaur Detective

Elephant's Everything Trunk

Use a paint marker to write *Elephant's Everything Trunk* on the side of a small trunk.

Alternative Theme Ideas

- Find fabric with an egg or elephant print, and use it to make a bag (see page 4).

- Find fabric with a print that shows several children, use it to make a bag (see page 4), and write *The Everybody Bag* along one side.

Literature Links

- ➥ *Animal Ears* by David M. Schwartz (Creative Teaching Press)
- ➥ *Edward the Emu* by Sheena Knowles (HarperCollins)
- ➥ *The Elephant's Ears* by Catherine Chambers (Barefoot Books)
- ➥ *Eleven Elephants Going Up* by Bethany Roberts and Patricia Hubbell (Whispering Coyote)
- ➥ *Elmer* by David McKee (Lothrop, Lee, & Shepard)

- ➥ *Engine, Engine, Number Nine* by Stephanie Calmenson (Hyperion Press)
- ➥ *An Extraordinary Egg* by Leo Lionni (Alfred A. Knopf Books)
- ➥ *Horton Hatches the Egg* by Dr. Seuss (Random House)
- ➥ *How to Catch an Elephant* by Amy Schwartz (DK Publishing)
- ➥ *It Started As an Egg* by Kimberlee Graves (Creative Teaching Press)

Playtime Props

- ★ elephant stuffed animal or puppet
- ★ elf figurine or costume
- ★ Ernie® or Elmo® doll
- ★ plastic eggs

Snacks to Sort, Sound Out, and Share

- ♥ Easter eggs
- ♥ Extra® gum

Elephant's Everything Trunk
Student Journal

Here are some of the things you can write in this journal.

1. Read one of the books in the kit, and write about your favorite part of the story.

2. Write your own story.

3. Write about what you think an elephant might pack in its trunk before it leaves for a trip.

4. List as many words as you can that begin with the letter e.

5. Write about your favorite game or activity in this kit. Tell why you liked it.

Remember: Always write your name before you write anything else in the journal!

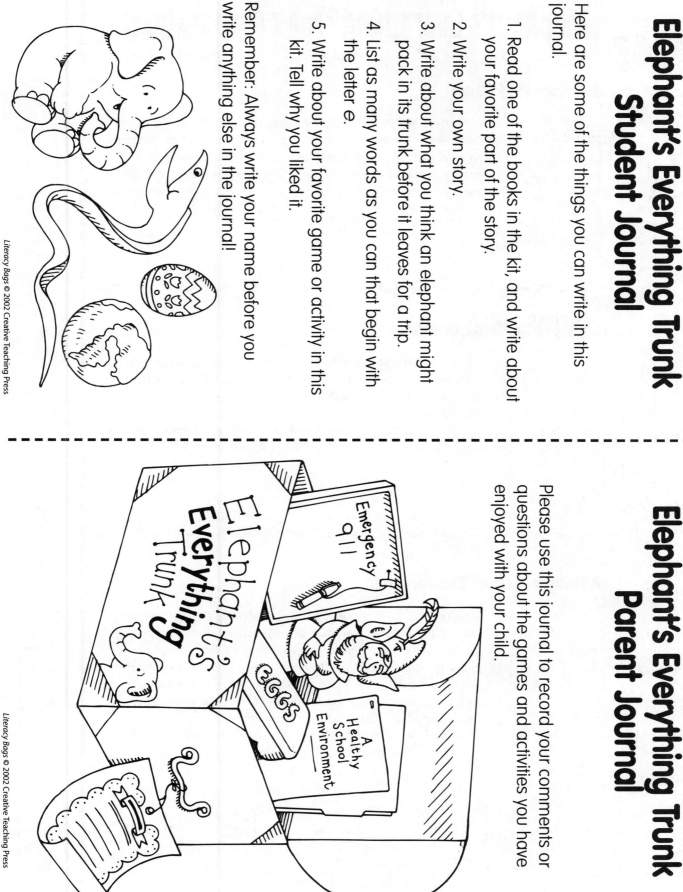

Elephant's Everything Trunk
Parent Journal

Please use this journal to record your comments or questions about the games and activities you have enjoyed with your child.

Elephant's Everything Trunk Preparations

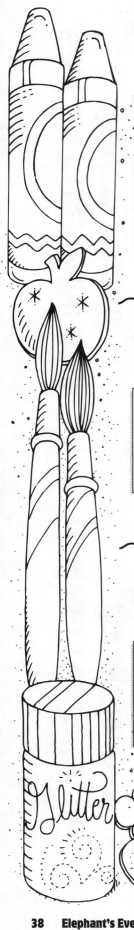

Egg Guessing Game

Children will identify beginning sounds.

Copy the **Egg Guessing Game Cards (page 40)** on **card stock,** color them, cut them apart and laminate them. Put the cards in **separate plastic eggs (one dozen),** and place the eggs in an **empty egg carton.** Tape the **Egg Guessing Game instruction card (page 39)** to the top of the carton, and place the carton in the kit.

Emergency Phone Numbers

Children will identify emergency phone numbers.

Use a **permanent marker** to write various emergency phone numbers, such as 911 and the local police and fire department numbers, at the top of a **dry erase board.** Tape the **Emergency Phone Numbers instruction card (page 39)** to the back of the board. Tie a piece of **string** to a **dry erase marker,** and tape it to the board. Place the board and a **toy phone** in the kit.

A Healthy School Environment

Children will identify healthy, positive aspects of their school environment.

Tape or glue the **A Healthy School Environment instruction card (page 39)** and a **picture of your school** to the front of a **file folder.** Open the folder. Write *Healthy Environment* at the top of the left side and *Unhealthy Environment* at the top of the right side, and laminate the folder. Attach six pieces of **Velcro®** to each side of the folder. Copy the **A Healthy School Environment Cards (page 41).** Color, cut apart, and laminate the cards. Attach a piece of Velcro to each card. Put the cards in a **resealable bag.** Place the bag and the folder in the kit.

Elephant's Everything Trunk Instruction Cards

Materials
- carton of plastic eggs

Egg Guessing Game

1. Remove an egg from the carton, and open it.
2. Look at the picture, and decide if the picture begins with *e*.
3. Replace the card in the egg, and set it aside.
4. Repeat the activity with the rest of the eggs.
5. Place the eggs back in the carton, and try to guess which eggs have a picture that begins with *e*.
6. Place the eggs back in the carton, and return the carton to the kit.

Materials
- dry erase board
- dry erase marker
- toy phone
- paper towel

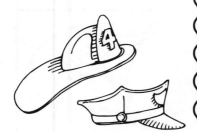

Emergency Phone Numbers

1. Read the phone numbers at the top of the board.
2. Use the special marker to circle the number for the police department.
3. Underline the number to the fire department.
4. Trace the 911 emergency number. Write the number 911 three more times.
5. Practice dialing the police, fire, and emergency numbers on the toy phone.
6. Use a damp paper towel to clean the board.
7. Return all items to the kit.

Materials
- A Healthy School Environment cards
- folder
- student journal

A Healthy School Environment

1. Remove the cards from the bag, and talk about the picture on each one.
2. If a card shows something that would be good for our school environment, place it on the "Healthy Environment" side of the folder. If a card shows something that would be bad for our school environment, place it on the "Unhealthy Environment" side of the folder.
3. Read the cards in each column.
4. Write or draw in the student journal something you will do to help make a healthy environment at school.
5. Remove the cards from the folder, and place them back in the bag.
6. Return all items to the kit.

Egg Guessing Game Cards

Literacy Bags © 2002 Creative Teaching Press

A Healthy School Environment Cards

Fun with Friends and Family

Find a print with people's faces, and use it to make a bag (see page 4). Use a fabric marker to write *Fun with Friends and Family* on one side.

Alternative Theme Ideas

- Find fabric with a fairy, farm, fish, flag, flower, fire engine, fox, frog, or foot print, and use it to make a bag (see page 4).

- Use a fishing tackle box.

Literature Links

- *Best Friends* by Sandi Hill (Creative Teaching Press)
- *Down on Casey's Farm* by Sandra Jordan (Orchard Books)
- *Families Share* by Rozanne Lanczak Williams (Creative Teaching Press)
- *Farming* by Gail Gibbons (Holiday House)
- *Feathers for Lunch* by Lois Ehlert (Harcourt)
- *Fish Eyes: A Book You Can Count On* by Lois Ehlert (Harcourt)
- *The Foot Book* by Dr. Seuss (Random House)
- *Freight Train* by Donald Crews (Mulberry Books)
- *Little Green Frog* by Rozanne Lanczak Williams (Creative Teaching Press)
- *The Rainbow Fish* by Marcus Pfister (North-South Books)

Playtime Props

★ cloth or plastic flowers
★ firefighter figure
★ fish, fox, or frog stuffed animals or puppets
★ Go Fish card game
★ toy farm/farm animals

Snacks to Sort, Sound Out, and Share

♥ Fruit by the Foot®
♥ Froot Loops® cereal
♥ Fruit Roll-Ups®
♥ goldfish crackers

Fun with Friends and Family
Student Journal

Here are some of the things you can write in this journal.

1. Read one of the books in the kit, and write about your favorite part of the story.

2. Write your own story.

3. Write about some of the ways you have fun with your friends and family.

4. List as many words as you can that begin with the letter *f*.

5. Write about your favorite game or activity in this kit. Tell why you liked it.

Remember: Always write your name before you write anything else in the journal!

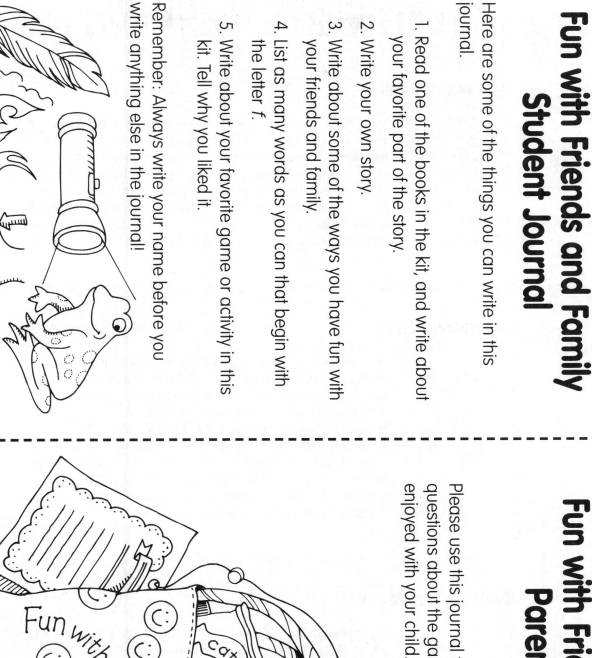

Fun with Friends and Family
Parent Journal

Please use this journal to record your comments or questions about the games and activities you have enjoyed with your child.

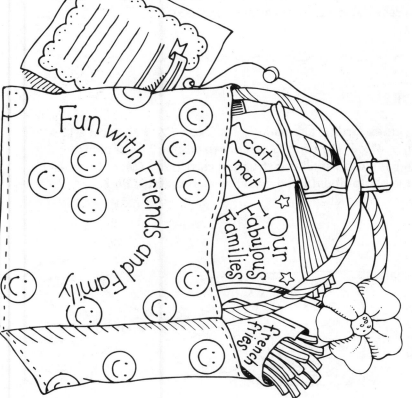

Fun with Friends and Family Preparations

Fish with a Friend

Children will identify and match rhyming words.

Make several copies of the **Fish reproducible (page 46)** on **card stock**, and cut out the fish. Write pairs of rhyming words on separate fish, and underline the rime in each word (e.g., *sat, cat, top, mop*). Laminate the fish, and attach a **paper clip** to each one. Place the fish and the **Fish with a Friend instruction card (page 45)** in a **resealable bag**. Tie a **magnet** to the end of a piece of **string**. Tie or tape the other end of the string to a **ruler or paint-stirring stick** to create a "fishing pole." Place all items in the kit.

French Fry Fun

Children will put numbers in ascending order and identify number words.

Color or paint **24 craft sticks yellow (or buy 24 yellow craft sticks)**. Write the number words for one through twelve on 12 of the sticks. Open a **file folder**. Glue sticks one through six to the left side and sticks seven through eight to the right side. Glue the **French Fry Fun instruction card (page 45)** to the front of the folder, and laminate it. Take another craft stick, draw one dot at one end, and write the numeral 1 at the other end. Repeat the process to make eleven more sticks for 2 through 12. Put these sticks in an **empty french fry container**, and place the container in a **resealable bag**. Place all items in the kit.

Our Fabulous Families

Children will write descriptions about their families.

Put **index cards** in alternating sleeves of a **3½" x 5" (9 cm x 12.5 cm)** or **4" x 6" (10 cm x 15 cm) photo album**. Tape or glue the **Our Fabulous Families instruction card (page 45)** to the cover of the photo album. Put the album in a **resealable bag**, and place it in the kit.

Fun with Friends and Family Instruction Cards

Materials
- fish cutouts
- "fishing pole"

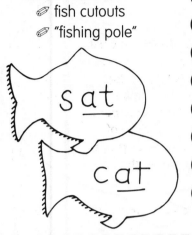

Fish with a Friend

1. Place the fish cutouts facedown on a flat surface.
2. Use the fishing pole to "catch" two fish.
3. Read the words on the fish. If the words rhyme, keep them. If the words do not rhyme, place them facedown again.
4. Keep fishing until you catch each pair of rhyming words.
5. Place the fish back in the bag, and return all items to the kit.

Materials
- container of "french fries"
- folder

French Fry Fun

1. Arrange the french fries in order from smallest to largest.
2. Open the folder. Place each french fry over its matching number word.
3. Replace the french fries in the container, and return all items to the kit.

Materials
- photo album

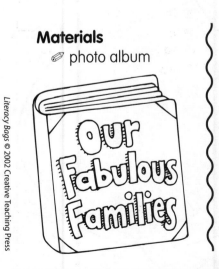

Our Fabulous Families

1. Find a photo of your family (or draw one if you do not have a photo available), and put it into an empty sleeve of the photo album.
2. Remove the index card that appears on the page below your family photo.
3. Write about your family. Include each person's name and age, and describe things he or she likes to do. Place the card back in the sleeve.
4. Read about some of the other families in the album.
5. Return the album to the kit.

Fish

Literacy Bags © 2002 Creative Teaching Press

Giraffe's Gym Bag

Find or make a yellow cloth bag, and use fabric paint to draw large brown spots on it. Use a fabric marker to write *Giraffe's Gym Bag* on one side.

Alternative Theme Ideas

- Find fabric with a gingerbread, giraffe, goat, goldfish, goose, gorilla, grapes, grasshopper, or gumball print, and use it to make a bag (see page 4).

- Use glitter fabric paint to write the words *Glittery Game Bag* on the side of any bag.

Literature Links

- *Boo to a Goose* by Mem Fox (Puffin)
- *Carlo Likes Reading* by Jessica Spanyol (Candlewick Press)
- *Curious George at the Airport* by Margaret Rey and Alan J. Shalleck (Houghton Mifflin)
- *The Giraffe Made Her Laugh* by Rozanne Lanczak Williams (Creative Teaching Press)
- *Good Night, Gorilla* by Peggy Rathmann (Putnam)
- *Goodnight Moon* by Margaret Wise Brown (Scholastic)
- *Grandmother's Garden* by John Archambault and David Plummer (Creative Teaching Press)
- *Out to Gumball Pond* by Margaret Allen (Creative Teaching Press)
- *Ten Tall Giraffes* by Brian Moses (Ladybird Books)
- *Where Are You Going?* by Kimberlee Graves and Rozanne Lanczak Williams (Creative Teaching Press)

Playtime Props

★ geo boards
★ G.I. Joe® dolls
★ giraffe, goat, goldfish, goose, grasshopper, or gorilla stuffed animals or puppets
★ glasses
★ glitter pens
★ golf balls

Snacks to Sort, Sound Out, and Share

♥ Fruit Gushers®
♥ goldfish crackers
♥ graham crackers
♥ gumballs

Giraffe's Gym Bag
Parent Journal

Please use this journal to record your comments or questions about the games and activities you have enjoyed with your child.

Giraffe's Gym Bag
Student Journal

Here are some of the things you can write in this journal.

1. Read one of the books in the kit, and write about your favorite part of the story.

2. Write your own story.

3. Write about what it would be like if your neck was as long as a giraffe's neck.

4. List as many words as you can that begin with the letter *g*.

5. Write about your favorite game or activity in this kit. Tell why you liked it.

Remember: Always write your name before you write anything else in the journal!

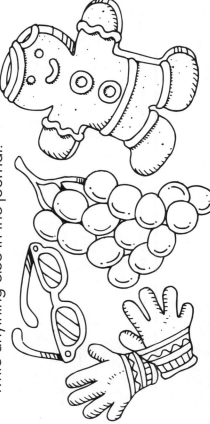

Giraffe's Gym Bag Preparations

Geometric Solids

Children will identify geometric solids.

Copy the **Geometric Solids reproducible (page 51)** on **card stock**, and laminate it. Put a **transparency marker**, a set of **geometric solids (sphere, cylinder, pyramid, cone, cube, rectangular prism)**, and the **Geometric Solids instruction card (page 50)** in a **resealable bag**. Place all items in the kit.

The Giraffe Game

Children will count, compare, and add sets of numbers from one to ten.

Copy the **Giraffe reproducible (page 52)** on a piece of **yellow card stock** and **orange card stock**. Cut out the giraffes, and laminate them. Cut eighteen 1" (2.5 cm) circles from **brown construction paper**, and put them in a **resealable bag**. Copy **The Giraffe Game Cards (page 53)**, and laminate them. Cut apart the cards, and place them and **The Giraffe Game instruction card (page 50)** in the bag. Place all items in the kit.

Gym Bag Aerobics

Children will measure their heart rate.

Put a **stopwatch, a stethoscope, assorted exercise equipment**, (e.g., **a jump rope, small balls/beanbags, whistle, small wrist weights, a children's exercise video—if desired**), and the **Gym Bag Aerobics instruction card (page 50)** in a **large resealable bag**. Place the bag in the kit.

Giraffe's Gym Bag Instruction Cards

Materials
- solid shapes
- Geometric Solids paper
- transparency marker
- student journal
- paper towel

Geometric Solids

1. Match each solid shape with the picture on the paper. Review the names of these solid shapes.
2. Look around your house for examples of these solid shapes. Use the special marker to write your answers on the paper.
3. Draw a picture of one or more of the solid shapes that you found in your house in the student journal.
4. Use a damp paper towel to clean the paper, and return all items to the kit.

Materials
- yellow and orange giraffes
- The Giraffe Game cards
- bag of small brown "spots"

The Giraffe Game

1. Place the giraffes side by side on a flat surface.
2. Place the cards facedown in a pile, and place the brown spots in a pile.
3. Choose a card, read it, and use the brown spots to follow the directions.
4. Count the spots on the giraffes to answer the question at the bottom of the card.
5. Remove the spots from both giraffes, and place the card at the bottom of the pile.
6. Choose a different card, and follow the new directions.
7. Repeat the process until you have completed the directions on all of the cards.
8. Place the spots and the cards back in the bag, and return all items to the kit.

Materials
- stopwatch
- student journal

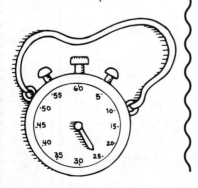

Gym Bag Aerobics

1. Place your hand over your heart, and ask someone to count to six silently. Count how many times your heart beats during those 6 seconds. Write the number in the student journal.
2. Ask someone to use the stopwatch to help you measure 1 minute. During that 1 minute, jog in place.
3. Place your hand over your heart again, ask someone to count to six silently, and count how many times your heart beats. Write this number in the journal.
4. Write or draw how you felt before and after you jogged for 1 minute.
5. Try another exercise, measure your heart rate, and write about it in the student journal.
6. Return all items to the kit.

Literacy Bags © 2002 Creative Teaching Press

Geometric Solids

Look at the shapes in this bag. Find an object in your house that matches each shape.

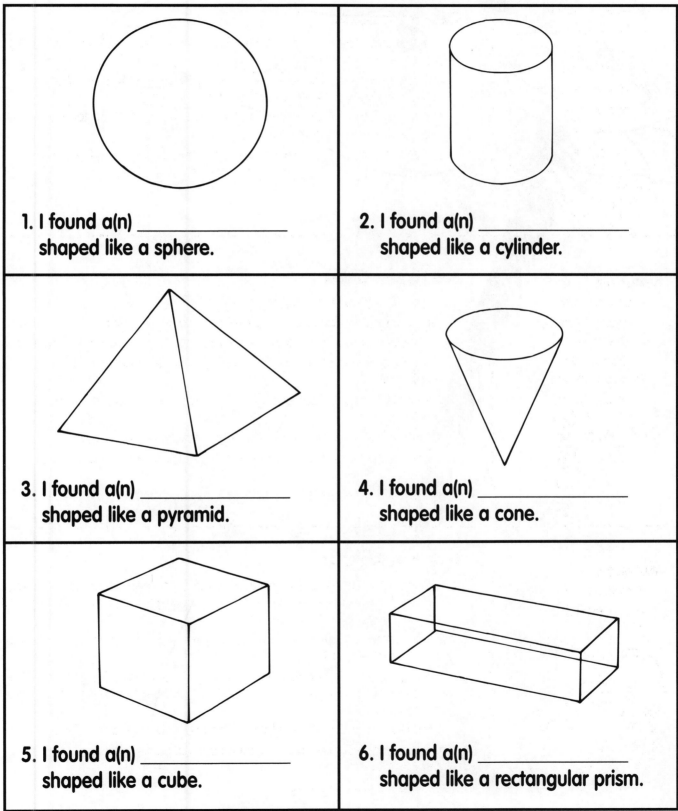

1. I found a(n) _____
   shaped like a sphere.

2. I found a(n) _____
   shaped like a cylinder.

3. I found a(n) _____
   shaped like a pyramid.

4. I found a(n) _____
   shaped like a cone.

5. I found a(n) _____
   shaped like a cube.

6. I found a(n) _____
   shaped like a rectangular prism.

Giraffe

The Giraffe Game Cards

Place two spots on the yellow giraffe.

Place three spots on the orange giraffe.

How many spots are there in all?

Place five spots on the yellow giraffe.

Place four spots on the orange giraffe.

Which giraffe has more spots?

Place seven spots on the yellow giraffe

Place one spot on the orange giraffe.

Which giraffe has more spots?

How many more spots does it have?

Place ten spots on the yellow giraffe.

Place five spots on the orange giraffe.

Which giraffe has less spots?

Place six spots on the yellow giraffe.

Place four spots on the orange giraffe.

How many spots are there in all?

Place nine spots on the yellow giraffe.

Place nine spots on the orange giraffe.

Which giraffe has more spots?

Happy Hearts Bag

Use fabric markers to draw hearts on a canvas bag. Use a fabric marker to write *Happy Hearts Bag* on one side of the bag.

Alternative Theme Ideas

- Find fabric with a hamburger, hammer, hand, hat, heart, helicopter, hippopotamus, horse, hot dog, or house print, and use it to make a bag (see page 4).

- Find fabric with a "happy birthday" print, and use it to make a bag (see page 4), or glue birthday candles to a box or other container.

- Use a Valentine's Day gift bag.

Literature Links

- ➡ *The Biggest House in the World* by Leo Lionni (Pantheon)
- ➡ *Happy Birthday, Dear Duck* by Eve Bunting (Clarion Books)
- ➡ *Happy Birthday, Moon* by Frank Asch (Simon & Schuster)
- ➡ *The Hippo Hop* by Christine Loomis (Houghton Mifflin)
- ➡ *Horses* by Cynthia F. Klingel (Child's World)
- ➡ *A House for Hermit Crab* by Eric Carle (Scholastic)
- ➡ *A House Is a House for Me* by Mary Ann Hoberman (Viking)
- ➡ *Mr. Noisy Builds a House* by Luella Connelly (Creative Teaching Press)
- ➡ *Mr. Noisy Paints His House* by Joel Kupperstein (Creative Teaching Press)
- ➡ *The Napping House* by Audrey Wood (Harcourt)

Playtime Props

★ harmonica
(clean with rubbing alcohol after each use)

★ hats

★ hippopotamus or horse stuffed animals or puppets

★ hopscotch mat

★ Hot Wheels® vehicles

★ plastic hamburgers or hot dogs

Snacks to Sort, Sound Out, and Share

♥ Hershey's® milk chocolate bar

♥ Hershey's® Kisses™

♥ Honeycomb® cereal

Happy Hearts Bag
Student Journal

Here are some of the things you can write in this journal.

1. Read one of the books in the kit, and write about your favorite part of the story.

2. Write your own story.

3. Write about someone who makes you happy.

4. List as many words as you can that begin with the letter *h*.

5. Write about your favorite game or activity in this kit. Tell why you liked it.

Remember: Always write your name before you write anything else in the journal!

Happy Hearts Bag
Parent Journal

Please use this journal to record your comments or questions about the games and activities you have enjoyed with your child.

Happy Hearts Bag Preparations

Home Is Where the Heart Is

Children will construct a house from blocks and draw it.

Put **small colored blocks or rods** and the **Home Is Where the Heart Is instruction card (page 57)** in a **resealable bag**. Put **colored pencils** in a separate resealable bag, and place the bags in the kit.

Hearts, Hearts, and More Hearts

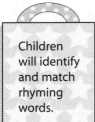

Children will identify and match rhyming words.

Make several copies of the **Hearts reproducible (page 58)** on **colored card stock**, and cut out the hearts. Write each word in a pair of rhyming words (e.g., see, tree; sun, fun) on separate hearts, and laminate them. Put the hearts and the **Hearts, Hearts, and More Hearts instruction card (page 57)** in a **resealable bag**, and place the bag in the kit. (Optional: Make a set of cards with pairs of uppercase and lowercase letters or numerals and number words instead.)

Get Your Hearts in Order

Children will arrange even numbers in ascending order.

Make two copies of the **Hearts reproducible (page 58)** on **colored card stock** (choose a different color than that used in the previous activity), and cut out the hearts. Write even numbers from 2 to 24 on separate hearts, and laminate them. Put the hearts and the **Get Your Hearts in Order instruction card (page 57)** in a **resealable bag**, and place the bag in the kit. (Optional: Make a set of cards with uppercase or lowercase letters, multiples of 5, multiples of 10, or odd numbers.)

Happy Hearts Bag Instruction Cards

Materials
- blocks or rods
- bag of colored pencils
- student journal

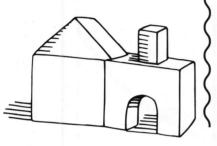

Home Is Where the Heart Is

1. Place the blocks or rods on a flat surface, and use them to build a house.
2. Draw in the student journal the house you built.
3. Place the blocks or rods and the colored pencils back in the bags, and return all items to the kit.

Materials
- heart cutouts

Hearts, Hearts, and More Hearts

1. Find someone to play this game with you.
2. Place the hearts facedown on a flat surface.
3. One player turns over two hearts. If the words on the cards rhyme, the player keeps the pair of hearts and plays again. If the words on the hearts do not rhyme, it is the next player's turn.
4. Play until no hearts remain.
5. Place the hearts back in the bag, and return it to the kit.

Materials
- heart cutouts

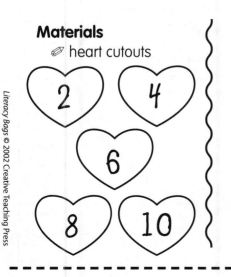

Get Your Hearts in Order

1. Place the hearts faceup on a flat surface, and read the numbers on them.
2. Arrange the hearts in order from smallest to largest.
3. Read the numbers on the hearts after you have put them in order.
4. Place the hearts back in the bag, and return it to the kit.

Hearts

Inchworm's Interesting Bag

Cut out several circles from felt of assorted colors, and glue them end-to-end on a canvas bag to make an inchworm. Use fabric paint to draw antennae, facial features, and feet on the inchworm and to write *Inchworm's Interesting Bag* on one side of the bag.

Alternative Theme Ideas

- Find fabric with an ice cream, iguana, inchworm, igloo, insect, or Native American Indian print, and use it to make a bag (see page 4).

- Use a large ice-cream container.

Literature Links

- *Alpha Bugs: A Pop-Up Alphabet* by David A. Carter (Simon & Schuster)
- *Curious George Goes to an Ice Cream Shop* by Margaret Rey and Alan J. Shalleck (Houghton Mifflin)
- *I Spy* by Margaret Allen (Creative Teaching Press)
- *Ice Cream Bear* by Jez Alborough (Candlewick Press)
- *Ice Cream Larry* by Daniel M. Pinkwater (Marshall Cavendish)

- *I'd Rather Have an Iguana* by Heidi Stetson Mario (Charlesbridge Publishing)
- *Inch by Inch* by Leo Lionni (Mulberry Books)
- *Inchworm and a Half* by Elinor Pinczes (Houghton Mifflin)
- *Insects and Crawly Creatures* by Angela Royston (Aladdin)
- *Ira Sleeps Over* by Bernard Waber (Houghton Mifflin)

Playtime Props

★ I Spy® game
★ iguana, inchworm, or insect stuffed animals or puppets
★ plastic insects

Snacks to Sort, Sound Out, and Share

♥ iced cookies
♥ Mike and Ike®

Inchworm's Interesting Bag
Parent Journal

Please use this journal to record your comments or questions about the games and activities you have enjoyed with your child.

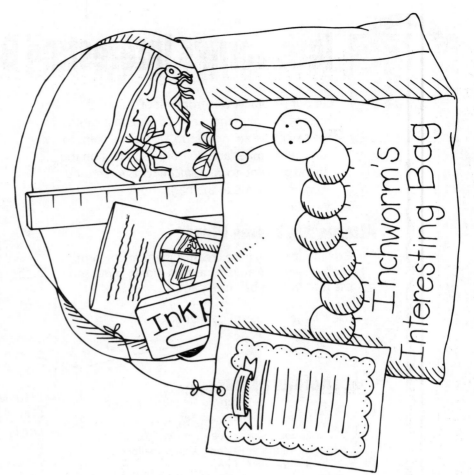

Literacy Bags © 2002 Creative Teaching Press

Inchworm's Interesting Bag
Student Journal

Here are some of the things you can write in this journal.

1. Read one of the books in the kit, and write about your favorite part of the story.

2. Write your own story.

3. Write about what you would keep in your own "interesting bag."

4. List as many words as you can that begin with the letter *i*.

5. Write about your favorite game or activity in this kit. Tell why you liked it.

Remember: Always write your name before you write anything else in the journal!

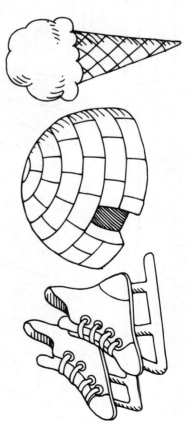

Literacy Bags © 2002 Creative Teaching Press

Inchworm's Interesting Bag Preparations

Inchworm Words

Children will identify and sort rhyming words.

Cut 16 circles from **colored card stock**. Draw facial features on four circles, and glue two **pipe cleaners** to the top of each of these four circles. Write the following rhyming words on separate circles: *bat, hat, sat, bet, get, net, dip, hip, ship, bug, jug,* and *rug.* Put the circles and the **Inchworm Words instruction card (page 62)** in a **resealable bag,** and place the bag in the kit.

Measuring in Inchworms

Children will measure in inches.

Copy the **Inchworm Measuring Tape reproducible (page 63)**. Cut out the strips, and glue them end to end in numerical order to make a measuring tape. Laminate the measuring tape, and put it with a **transparency marker** and the **Measuring in Inchworms instruction card (page 62)** in a **resealable bag.** Copy the **Measuring in Inchworms reproducible (page 64)** on **card stock**, laminate it, and place it in the bag. Place the bag in the kit.

Ink Pad Insects

Children will create thumbprint insects.

Put an **ink pad**, **markers**, and the **Ink Pad Insects instruction card (page 62)** in a **resealable bag**, and place the bag in the kit.

Inchworm's Interesting Bag Instruction Cards

Materials
- circle cutouts
- student journal

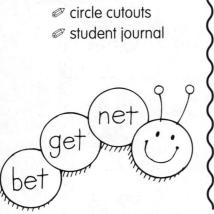

Inchworm Words

1. Place the four circle "heads" in a pile.
2. Sort the circles into groups of rhyming words, and connect a head to each set of circles to make four rhyming-word "inchworms."
3. Write one group of rhyming words in the student journal. Think of other words that rhyme with the words on your list, and write them in the journal.
4. Place the circles back in the bag, and return all items to the kit.

Materials
- Measuring in Inchworms paper
- inchworm measuring tape
- transparency marker
- paper towel

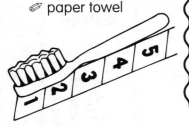

Measuring in Inchworms

1. Read the Measuring in Inchworms paper.
2. Use the inchworm measuring tape to measure the items listed on the paper.
3. Use the special marker to write your answers on the paper.
4. Ask someone to check your work.
5. Use a damp paper towel to wipe away your work.
6. Return all items to the kit.

Materials
- student journal
- ink pad
- markers

Ink Pad Insects

1. Open the student journal to a new page.
2. Press your thumb on the ink pad, and then press your thumb on the journal page.
3. Use the markers to draw a face, antennae, legs, and other features on your thumbprint to create an "insect."
4. Think of a name for your insect, and write it in the journal.
5. Write a story about your insect.
6. If you have time, make some other insects, and write stories about them.
7. Return all items to the kit.

Inchworm Measuring Tape

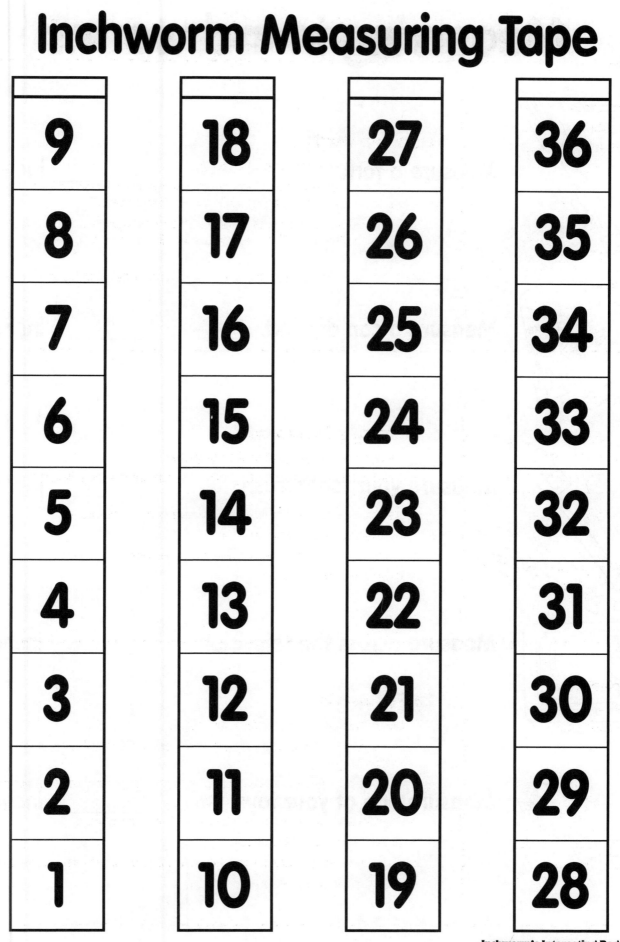

9	18	27	36
8	17	26	35
7	16	25	34
6	15	24	33
5	14	23	32
4	13	22	31
3	12	21	30
2	11	20	29
1	10	19	28

Measuring in Inchworms

 Measure a fork.   _____ inches

 Measure a can of food.   _____ inches

 Measure your toothbrush.   _____ inches

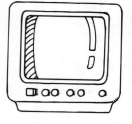 Measure across the television.   _____ inches

 Measure one of your toys.   _____ inches

Jammin' Jungle Bag

Find a khaki-colored or camouflage-print bag, and use a fabric marker to write *Jammin' Jungle Bag* on one side.

Alternative Theme Ideas

- Find fabric with a Jack and the Beanstalk, jacket, jaguar, jelly bean, jellyfish, jet, juggling, or jungle print, and use it to make a bag (see page 4).

- Glue rhinestones and sequins to a denim bag, and use a fabric marker to write *Jazzy Bag* on one side.

- Cover an empty detergent box with light blue paper. Cut out clouds from white construction paper, and glue them to the box. Attach airplane stickers to the box, and use a marker to write *Jumbo Jet Adventure* on one side of it.

Literature Links

- ➥ *The Animal Boogie* by Debbie Harter (Barefoot Books)
- ➥ *The Giant Jam Sandwich* by John Vernon Lord and Janet Burroway (Houghton Mifflin)
- ➥ *The Jacket I Wear in the Snow* by Shirley Neitzel (Greenwillow Books)
- ➥ *Jamberry* by Bruce Degen (HarperCollins)
- ➥ *Jesse Bear, What Will You Wear?* by Nancy White Carlston (Aladdin)

- ➥ *The Jester Has Lost His Jingle* by David Saltzman (Jester Company)
- ➥ *Jet It, Get It* by Margaret Allen (Creative Teaching Press)
- ➥ *The Jigaree* by Joy Cowley (The Wright Group)
- ➥ *Sheep in a Jeep* by Nancy Shaw (Houghton Mifflin)
- ➥ *Stripe* by Joanne Partis (Carolrhoda Books)

Playtime Props

★ jacks

★ jaguar, jellyfish, or jungle animal stuffed animals or puppets

★ Jenga®

★ jigsaw puzzles

★ jingle bells

★ jump ropes

★ toy jeeps

★ toy jet airplanes

Snacks to Sort, Sound Out, and Share

♥ Apple Jacks® cereal

♥ jelly beans

♥ Jolly Ranchers®

Jammin' Jungle Bag
Parent Journal

Please use this journal to record your comments or questions about the games and activities you have enjoyed with your child.

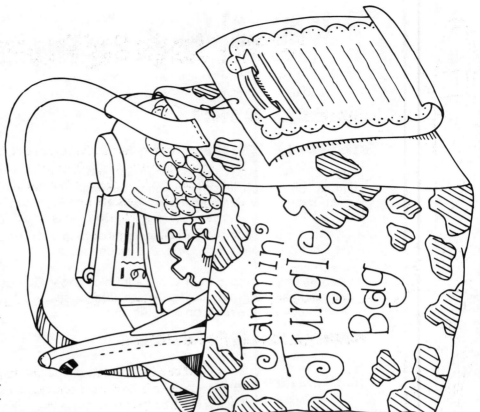

Jammin' Jungle Bag
Student Journal

Here are some of the things you can write in this journal.

1. Read one of the books in the kit, and write about your favorite part of the story.

2. Write your own story.

3. Imagine that you played along with a jungle band, and write about it.

4. List as many words as you can that begin with the letter *j*.

5. Write about your favorite game or activity in this kit. Tell why you liked it.

Remember: Always write your name before you write anything else in the journal!

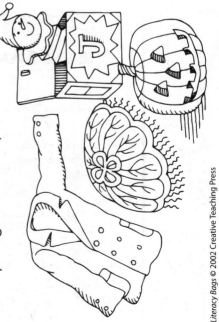

Jammin' Jungle Bag Preparations

Jammin' Jungle Beat

Children will copy and create rhythmic patterns.

Copy the **Jammin' Jungle Beat reproducible (page 69)** on **card stock**, and laminate it. Place the Jammin' Jungle Beat reproducible and the **Jammin' Jungle Beat instruction card (page 68)** in a **resealable bag**. Place the bag, **simple rhythm instruments (e.g., rhythm sticks, small drum, tambourine)**, and **cassettes and a cassette player** (if desired) in the kit.

Kindergarten Jungle Adventure

Children will write an original story.

Ask a child or a small group of children to pretend that they are exploring a jungle, and use a **camera** to take a picture of them. Tell the children that they can imitate climbing a tree, looking under a bush, or riding an animal. Take enough pictures so that each child in class appears in one. Develop the pictures, and tape each picture to a separate piece of **blank paper**. Put each paper in a **vinyl sheet protector**, and place each sheet protector in a **binder**. Hole-punch several sheets of blank paper, and put them in the back of the binder. Tape the **Kindergarten Jungle Adventure instruction card (page 68)** to the cover of the binder, and place it in the kit.

Jungle Jigsaw Puzzles

Children will spell simple verbs.

Copy the **Jungle Jigsaw Puzzles reproducibles (pages 70–71)** on **card stock**, cut apart the puzzle pieces, and laminate them. Put the puzzle pieces and the **Jungle Jigsaw Puzzles instruction card (page 68)** in a **resealable bag**, and place the bag in the kit.

Jammin' Jungle Bag Instruction Cards

Materials

- Jammin' Jungle Beat paper
- simple instruments
- cassette/cassette player (optional)

Jammin' Jungle Beat

1. Look at the Jammin' Jungle Beat paper. Each mark on the paper represents a beat.
2. Choose an instrument, and use it to play one of the patterns on the paper.
3. Choose another instrument or pattern, and repeat the activity.
4. If you want, play a cassette, and follow the beat of the song with an instrument.
5. Return all items to the kit.

Materials

- Kindergarten Jungle Adventure binder

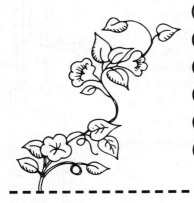

Kindergarten Jungle Adventure

1. Remove a blank page from the binder.
2. Find your picture in the binder.
3. Write a story about what you are doing in the picture. Try to answer these questions in your story: What animals did you see? What was the weather like? What did you eat? Where did you sleep? How did you feel?
4. Put your story in the binder behind your picture.
5. Return all items to the kit.

Materials

- puzzle pieces

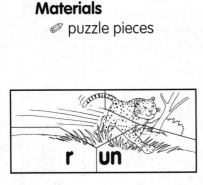

Jungle Jigsaw Puzzles

1. Place the puzzle pieces on a flat surface.
2. Put together the pieces to make six different puzzles.
3. Read the words on the puzzles.
4. Imitate the actions of the animals in the puzzles.
5. Place all the pieces back in the bag, and return all items to the kit.

Jammin' Jungle Beat

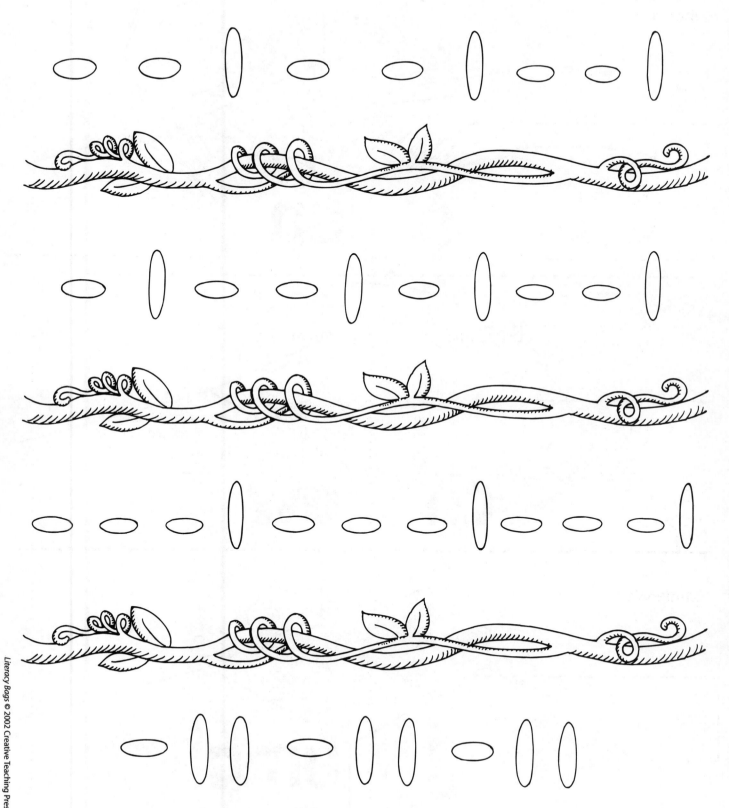

Jungle Jigsaw Puzzles

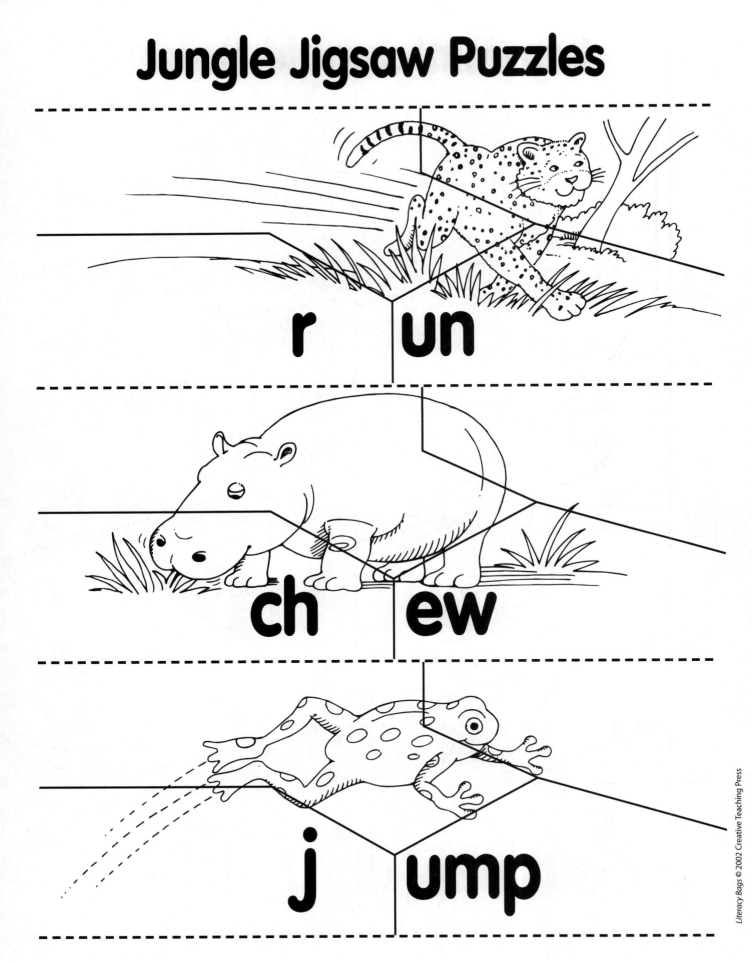

r | un

ch | ew

j | ump

Jungle Jigsaw Puzzles

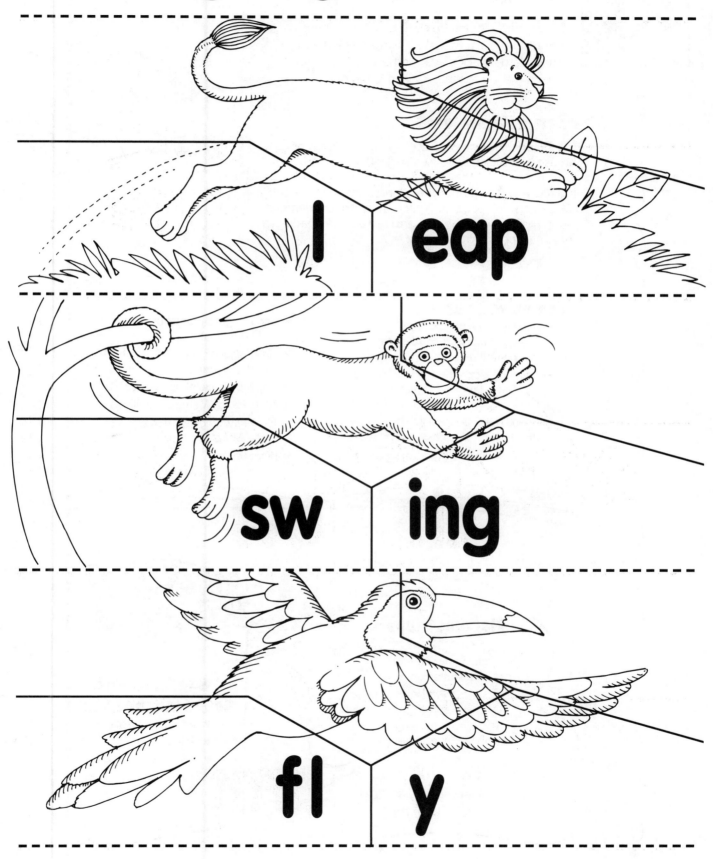

l eap

sw ing

fl y

Kitchen Kit

Find fabric with a tablecloth or kitchen-utensils print, and use it to make a bag (see page 4), or use a large black plastic kettle. Use a fabric or paint marker to write *Kitchen Kit* on one side.

Alternative Theme Ideas

- Find a fabric with a kangaroo, key, kite, or kitten print, and use it to make a bag (see page 4).

- Find red velvet or fabric with a king print, and use it to make a bag (see page 4). Attach shiny gold garland or ribbon to the top of the bag, and use a fabric marker to write *The King's Kit* on one side of it.

Literature Links

- ➥ *A Beautiful Feast for a Big King Cat* by John Archambault and Bill Martin Jr. (HarperCollins)
- ➥ *Counting Kittens* by John Archambault and David Plummer (Creative Teaching Press)
- ➥ *Curious George Flies a Kite* by Margaret Rey (Houghton Mifflin)
- ➥ *Does A Kangaroo Have a Mother, Too?* by Eric Carle (HarperCollins)
- ➥ *Good Knight* by Linda Rymill (Henry Holt and Company)
- ➥ *King Bidgood's in the Bathtub* by Audrey Wood (Harcourt)
- ➥ *Kipper* by Mick Inkpen (Harcourt)
- ➥ *Koala Lou* by Mem Fox (Gulliver)
- ➥ *Too Many Kangaroo Things to Do!* by Stuart Murphy (HarperCollins)
- ➥ *What Do You Do with a Kangaroo?* by Mercer Mayer (Scholastic)

Playtime Props
★ kaleidoscope
★ kangaroo, king, or kitten stuffed animals or puppets
★ kazoo (clean with rubbing alcohol after each use)
★ kite
★ Koosh® ball
★ lock and key

Snacks to Sort, Sound Out, and Share
♥ Hershey's® Kisses™
♥ Kit Kat®
♥ Kix® cereal

Kitchen Kit
Student Journal

Here are some of the things you can write in this journal.

1. Read one of the books in the kit, and write about your favorite part of the story.

2. Write your own story.

3. Write about the things that you and your family do in your kitchen.

4. List as many words as you can that begin with the letter k.

5. Write about your favorite game or activity in this kit. Tell why you liked it.

Remember: Always write your name before you write anything else in the journal!

Kitchen Kit
Parent Journal

Please use this journal to record your comments or questions about the games and activities you have enjoyed with your child.

KITCHEN KIT

Kitchen Kit Parent Journal

Kitchen Kit Preparations

Kitchen Counting

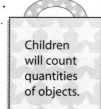

Children will count quantities of objects.

Copy the **Kitchen Counting reproducible (page 76)** on **card stock**, and laminate it. Put a **transparency marker** and the **Kitchen Counting instruction card (page 75)** in a **resealable bag**. Place all items in the kit.

Kitchen Magnet Match-Up

Children will identify and match rhyming words.

Copy the **Kitchen Magnet Match-Up reproducible (page 77)** on **card stock**, color the cards, and cut them apart. Laminate the cards, and attach a piece of **magnetic tape** to the back of each card. Put the cards and the **Kitchen Magnet Match-Up instruction card (page 75)** in a **resealable bag**, and place the bag in the kit.

The King's Kitchen

Children will write a story.

Tape **The King's Kitchen instruction card (page 75)** to the cover of a **file folder**. Put a piece of **paper** for each child in the file folder, and place the folder in the kit. When each child has completed this activity, bind children's papers together in a class book titled *A Visit to the King's Kitchen*.

Kitchen Kit Instruction Cards

Materials

- Kitchen Counting paper
- transparency marker
- paper towel

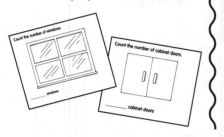

Kitchen Counting

1. Have a seat at your kitchen table.
2. Read the Kitchen Counting paper, and follow the directions. Use the special marker to write your answers on the paper.
3. Use a damp paper towel to clean your work, and return all items to the kit.

Materials

- Kitchen Magnet Match-Up cards
- student journal
- cookie sheet (optional)

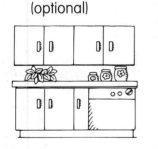

Kitchen Magnet Match-Up

1. Place the cards on your refrigerator or a cookie sheet.
2. Match the rhyming words.
3. Choose a pair of rhyming words, and write them in the student journal. Write other words that rhyme with this pair of words.
4. Place the cards back in the bag.
5. Return all items to the kit.

Materials

- folder
- crayons or markers

The King's Kitchen

1. Imagine that you have been invited to a royal kitchen to have dinner with the king.
2. Remove a piece of paper from the folder. Draw a picture of you and the king eating dinner.
3. Write a story about what it was like eating dinner with the king. Remember to describe what you ate and what you talked about.
4. Place your paper back in the folder, and return the folder to the kit.

Kitchen Counting

Count the number of windows.

_____ windows

Count the number of cabinet doors.

_____ cabinet doors

Count the number of handles on the cabinet doors.

_____ handles

Count the number of legs on the table.

_____ legs

Count the number of chairs at the table.

_____ chairs

Count the total number of legs on all the chairs.

_____ chair legs

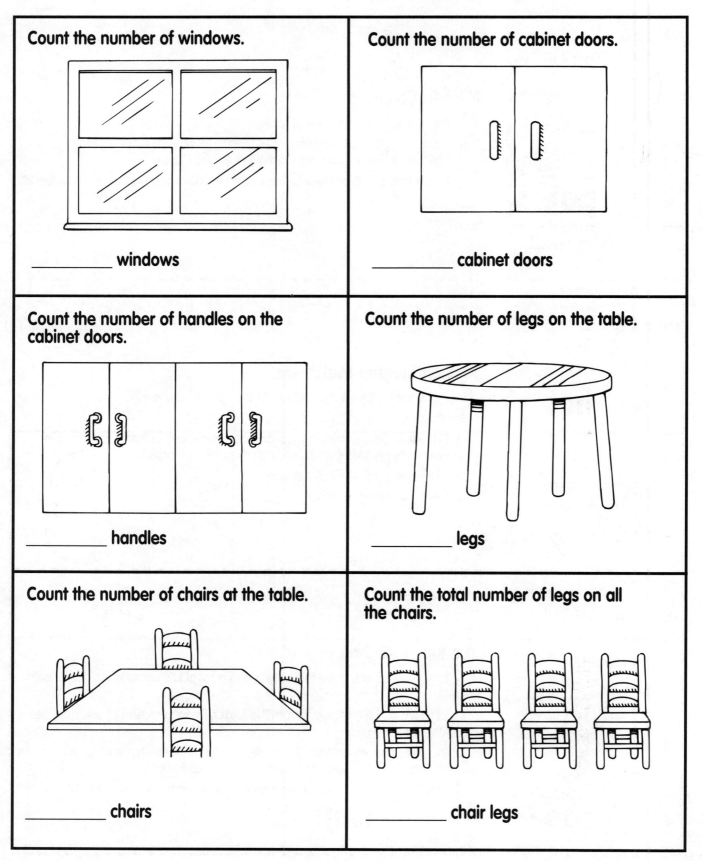

Literacy Bags © 2002 Creative Teaching Press

Kitchen Magnet Match-Up

pot

jam

dish

hot

ham

fish

pan

drink

chip

can

sink

dip

Ladybug's Luggage

Use red cloth to make a bag (see page 4), or use a red bag. Use a black fabric marker to draw black spots on it and to write *Ladybug's Luggage* on one side.

Alternative Theme Ideas

- Find fabric with a ladybug, lamb, ladder, leopard, leaf, lightning, lion, llama, lollipop, or lunch box print, and use it to make a bag (see page 4).

- Use a lunch box.

- Use a plastic Lego® container with a lid and a handle.

Literature Links

- *Are You a Ladybug?* by Judy Allen and Tudor Humphries (Kingfisher Books)
- *The Grouchy Ladybug* by Eric Carle (HarperCollins)
- *I Like Me* by Nancy Carlson (Puffin)
- *Is Your Mama a Llama?* by Deborah Guarino (Scholastic)
- *Leo the Late Bloomer* by Robert Kraus (Simon & Schuster)
- *Lovable Lyle* by Bernard Waber (Houghton Mifflin)
- *Lunch* by Denise Fleming (Henry Holt and Company)
- *Lyle, Lyle Crocodile* by Bernard Waber (Houghton Mifflin)
- *Mary Had a Little Lamb* by Sarah J. Hale (Scholastic)
- *The Very Lazy Ladybug* by Isobel Finn (Little Tiger Press)

Playtime Props
★ ladybug, lamb, lion, or llama stuffed animals or puppets
★ lacing cards
★ Legos®
★ linking cubes

Snacks to Sort, Sound Out, and Share
♥ Laffy Taffy®
♥ Lemonheads®
♥ licorice
♥ Life® cereal
♥ Lifesavers®
♥ lollipops
♥ Lucky Charms® cereal

Ladybug's Luggage
Student Journal

Here are some of the things you can write in this journal.

1. Read one of the books in the kit, and write about your favorite part of the story.

2. Write your own story.

3. Write about a trip you have taken or would like to take.

4. List as many words as you can that begin with the letter *l*.

5. Write about your favorite game or activity in this kit. Tell why you liked it.

Remember: Always write your name before you write anything else in the journal!

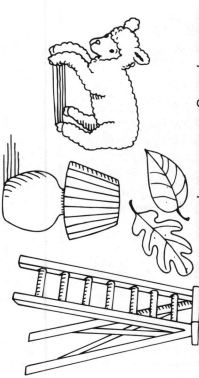

Ladybug's Luggage
Parent Journal

Please use this journal to record your comments or questions about the games and activities you have enjoyed with your child.

Ladybug's Luggage Preparations

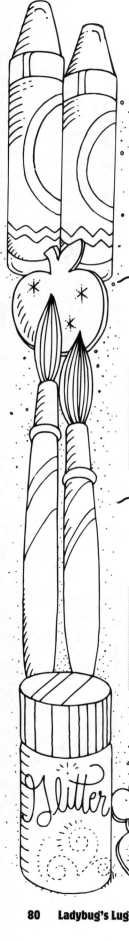

Leaping Ladybug!

Children will identify ordinal numbers.

Copy the **Leaping Ladybug! reproducible (page 82)** on **card stock**, color it, and laminate it. Copy the ladybug on the **Leaping Ladybug! instruction card (page 81)**, color it, cut it out, and laminate it. Attach a piece of **magnetic tape** to each leaf on the reproducible and to the back of the ladybug cutout. Put the ladybug cutout and the instruction card in a **resealable bag**, and place all items in the kit.

Living/Nonliving

Children will classify living and nonliving things.

Open a **file folder**, and write *Living* at the top of the left side and *Nonliving* at the top of the right side. Tape the **Living/Nonliving instruction card (page 81)** to the cover of the file folder, and laminate it. Copy the **Living/Nonliving Cards (page 83)** on **card stock**, cut them apart, and laminate them. Put the cards in a **resealable bag**, and place the bag and the folder in the kit.

Listen with Your Little Ears

Children will follow auditory directions.

Make a class set of the **Listen with Your Little Ears reproducible (page 84)**, and place them in a **file folder**. Record the following directions on a **cassette tape**. Pause between each command.

Color the ladybug's spots black.
Color the ladybug's body red.
Color the ladybug's head black.
Draw a circle around the entire ladybug.
Draw an X above the ladybug's head.

Put **crayons** and the **Listen with Your Little Ears instruction card (page 81)** in a **resealable bag**. Place all items in the kit.

Ladybug's Luggage Instruction Cards

Materials
- Leaping Ladybug! paper
- ladybug cutout

Leaping Ladybug!

1. Place the Leaping Ladybug! paper on a flat surface.
2. Use the ladybug cutout to follow the directions at the bottom of the paper.
3. Place the cutout back in the bag, and return all items to the kit.

Materials
- Living/Nonliving folder
- Living/Nonliving cards
- student journal

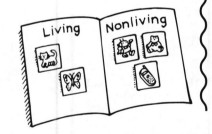

Living/Nonliving

1. Decide which cards show things that are living, and place them under "Living."
2. Decide which cards show things that are nonliving, and place them under "Nonliving."
3. Think of a few other examples of living and nonliving things, and list them in the student journal.
4. Place the cards back in the bag, and return all items to the kit.

Materials
- Listen with Your Little Ears folder
- cassette/cassette player
- bag of crayons

Listen with Your Little Ears

1. Write your name at the top of a Listen with Your Little Ears paper.
2. Play the cassette tape, and follow the directions that you hear.
3. Place your paper back in the folder and the crayons in the bag, and return all items to the kit.

Literacy Bags © 2002 Creative Teaching Press

Leaping Ladybug!

Place the ladybug on the second leaf.

Place the ladybug on the middle leaf.

Place the ladybug on the fifth leaf.

Place the ladybug on the first leaf.

Place the ladybug on the last leaf.

Place the ladybug on the third leaf.

Literacy Bags © 2002 Creative Teaching Press

Living/Nonliving Cards

Literacy Bags © 2002 Creative Teaching Press

Listen with Your Little Ears

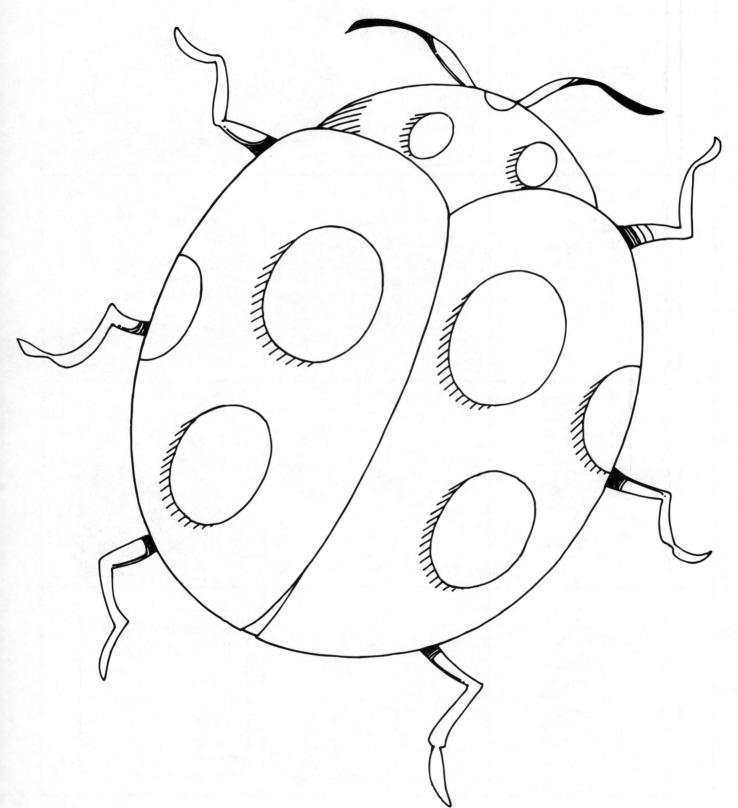

Making Magic

Cover a box with dark paper. Attach sparkly or glow-in-the-dark star and moon stickers to the box, and use a paint marker to write *Making Magic* on one side.

Alternative Theme Ideas

- Find fabric with a marble, mail, mitten, monkey, moon, moose, mouse, or muffin print, and use it to make a bag (see page 4).

- Paint black hair and facial features on a large green bucket. Use a paint marker to write *Monster Materials* on one side of it.

Literature Links

- *Five Little Monkeys Jumping on the Bed* by Elieen Christelow (Clarion Books)
- *Go Away, Big Green Monster* by Ed Emberley (Little, Brown and Company)
- *If You Give a Moose a Muffin* by Laura Joffe Numeroff (HarperCollins)
- *The Magic Money Box* by Rozanne Lanczak Williams (Creative Teaching Press)
- *Magical, Miracle Me* by John Archambault and David Plummer (Creative Teaching Press)
- *Matthew the Magician* by Kimberlee Graves (Creative Teaching Press)
- *Meanies* by Joy Cowley (The Wright Group)
- *Mouse Count* by Ellen Stoll Walsh (Harcourt)
- *Mouse Magic* by Ellen Stoll Walsh (Harcourt)
- *Mrs. Brice's Mice* by Syd Hoff (HarperTrophy)

Playtime Props
- ★ magnets
- ★ marbles
- ★ Memory® game
- ★ Mickey® or Minnie Mouse® dolls
- ★ mittens
- ★ monkey, moose, or mouse stuffed animals or puppets
- ★ Monopoly Jr.® game
- ★ musical instruments

Snacks to Sort, Sound Out, and Share
- ♥ M&M's®
- ♥ marshmallows
- ♥ Disney's® Mickey and Friends fruit snacks

Making Magic Parent Journal

Please use this journal to record your comments or questions about the games and activities you have enjoyed with your child.

Making Magic Student Journal

Here are some of the things you can write in this journal.

1. Read one of the books in the kit, and write about your favorite part of the story.

2. Write your own story.

3. Write about what you would do if you had magical powers.

4. List as many words as you can that begin with the letter *m*.

5. Write about your favorite game or activity in this kit. Tell why you liked it.

Remember: Always write your name before you write anything else in the journal!

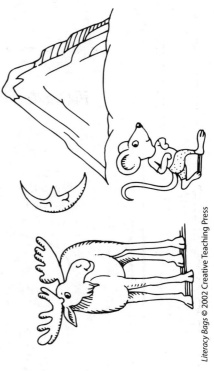

Making Magic Preparations

Magical Masks

Children will decorate a mask.

Copy the **Magical Mask reproducible (page 89)** on **card stock** for each child, and place the masks in a **file folder**. Glue the **Magical Masks instruction card (page 88)** to the cover of the folder. Cut two pieces of **yarn or string** for each mask. Put the pieces of yarn or string and **decorative objects (e.g., sequins, buttons, confetti, colored macaroni)** in a **resealable bag**. Place all items in the kit.

Me in the Mirror

Children will draw a self-portrait.

Copy the **Me in the Mirror reproducible (page 90)** for each child, and place the papers in a **file folder**. Glue the **Me in the Mirror instruction card (page 88)** to the cover of the folder. Put a **hand mirror** and **colored pencils** in a **resealable bag**. Place all items in the kit.

Make 'Em Disappear

Children will practice subtraction of quantities less than ten.

Copy the **Make 'Em Disappear reproducible (page 91)** for each child, and place the papers in a **file folder**. Glue the **Make 'Em Disappear instruction card (page 88)** to the cover. Put ten **M&M's® or mini-marshmallows** in a **resealable bag**. Place all items in the kit.

Making Magic Instruction Cards

Materials

- folder
- scissors
- yarn or string
- crayons
- glue
- decorative objects (e.g., sequins, buttons, confetti, colored macaroni)

Magical Masks

1. Remove one mask from the folder, and cut out the mask and the eyeholes.
2. Ask someone to help you make a slit on each side of the mask. Tie a piece of yarn or string through each of these slits.
3. Color your mask, and glue some of the decorative objects on it.
4. After the glue dries, wear the mask as you complete some of the other activities in this kit.
5. Return all items (except your mask) to the kit.

Materials

- folder
- hand mirror
- colored pencils

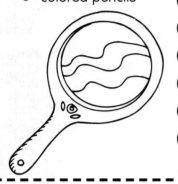

Me in the Mirror

1. Remove a paper from the folder.
2. Remove your mask from your face if you are wearing it now.
3. Look in the mirror, and examine your face.
4. Draw on your paper what you see in the mirror.
5. Place your paper back in the folder, and return all items to the kit.

Materials

- folder
- bag of snacks

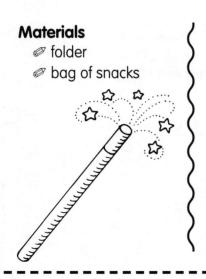

Make 'Em Disappear

1. Remove a paper from the folder, and place it on a flat surface.
2. Remove the snacks from the bag, and place one snack on each star on the paper.
3. Read the poem, and follow the directions.
4. Continue the activity until no snacks remain.
5. Return the folder and the instruction card to the kit.

Literacy Bags © 2002 Creative Teaching Press

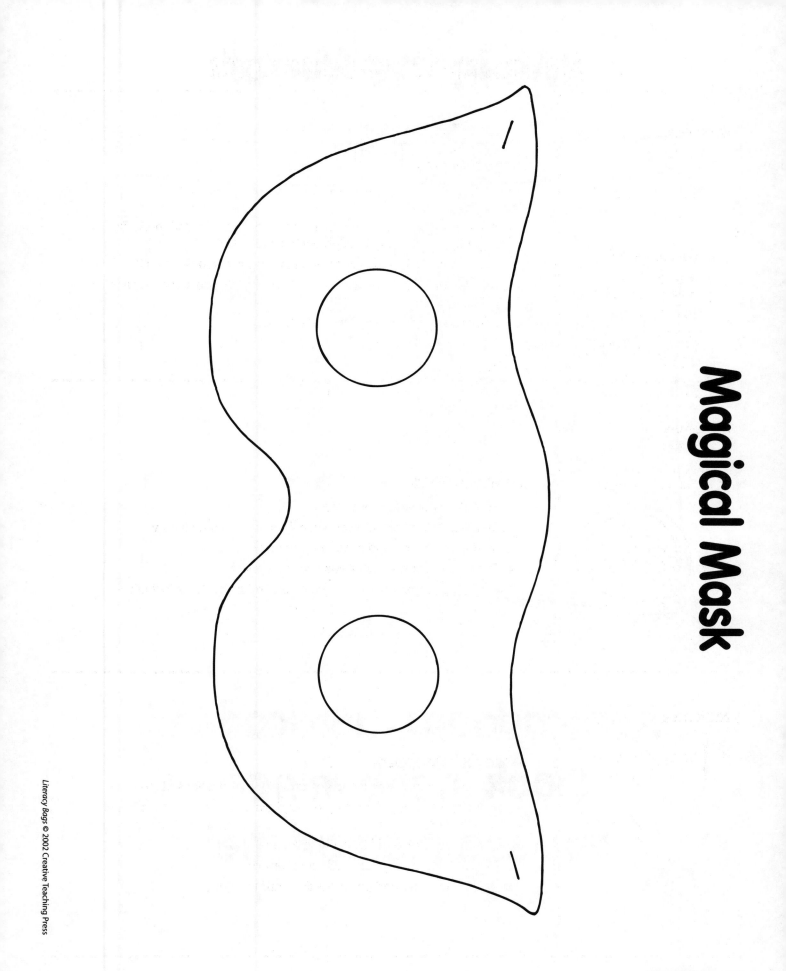

Magical Mask

Me in the Mirror

Abracadabra, abracadee.
I look in the mirror
and see magical me!

Make 'Em Disappear

I, the marvelous math magician,
Will do a trick with this group of ten.

Abracadabra, kalamazine.
I eat just one—and now there are nine.

Abracadabra, kalamazate.
I eat just one—and now there are eight.

Abracadabra, kalamazeven.
I eat just one—and now there are seven.

Abracadabra, kalamazix.
I eat just one—and now there are six.

Abracadabra, kalamazive.
I eat just one—and now there are five.

Abracadabra, kalamazor.
I eat just one—and now there are four.

Abracadabra, kalamazee.
I eat just one—and now there are three.

Abracadabra, kalamazoo.
I eat just one—and now there are two.

Abracadabra, kalamazun.
I eat just one—and now there is one.

Abracadabra, kalamazear.
One by one I made my snacks disappear!

Number Fun Notebook

Find a binder that zips closed. Use a fabric marker to write *Number Fun Notebook* on the cover.

Alternative Theme Ideas

- Find fabric with a nest, neighborhood, night, nurse, or nursery rhyme print, and use it to make a bag (see page 4).

- Cover a box with plain contact paper, attach number stickers to it, and use a paint marker to write *Name the Numbers Box* on one side.

Literature Links

- *Colors, Shapes, Words, and Numbers* by Alan Snow (Children's Press)
- *Little Number Stories: Addition* by Rozanne Lanczak Williams (Creative Teaching Press)
- *Little Number Stories: Subtraction* by Rozanne Lanczak Williams (Creative Teaching *Press*)
- *Mr. Noisy's Book of Patterns* by Rozanne Lanczak Williams (Creative Teaching Press)
- *The Napping House* by Audrey Wood (Harcourt)
- *Never Talk to Strangers* by Irma Joyce (Golden Books)
- *Newt* by Matt Novak (HarperCollins)
- *No, No, Nicky* by Rozanne Lanczak Williams (Creative Teaching Press)
- *Numbers All around Me* by Trisha Callella-Jones (Creative Teaching Press)
- *Underwater Counting: Even Numbers* by Jerry Pallotta (Charlesbridge Publishing)

Playtime Props

★ necklace
★ net
★ newt stuffed animal or puppet
★ number lacing cards
★ nurse's kit

Snacks to Sort, Sound Out, and Share

♥ Fig Newtons®
♥ Nerds®
♥ Nestlé® Crunch®
♥ nuts
♥ Nutter Butter® cookies

Number Fun Notebook
Student Journal

Here are some of the things you can write in this journal.

1. Read one of the books in the kit, and write about your favorite part of the story.

2. Write your own story.

3. Describe some things you see that have numbers on them.

4. List as many words as you can that begin with the letter n.

5. Write about your favorite game or activity in this kit. Tell why you liked it.

Remember: Always write your name before you write anything else in the journal!

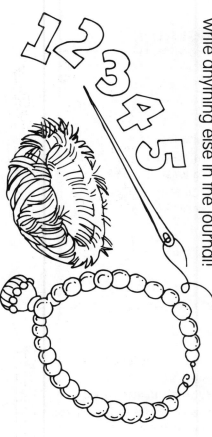

Number Fun Notebook
Parent Journal

Please use this journal to record your comments or questions about the games and activities you have enjoyed with your child.

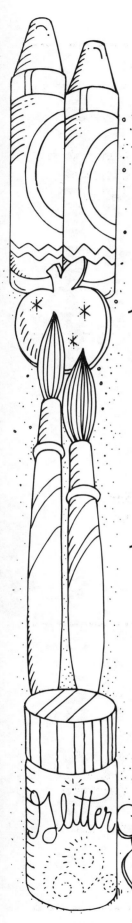

Number Fun Notebook Preparations

Number Necklaces

Children will put numbers in ascending order.

Choose a set of numbers (e.g., 1–10, 1–20, multiples of 5, multiples of 10). Write each number on a separate **lacing bead**. Put the beads in a **resealable bag**. Tie a **washer** to the end of a **shoestring or piece of yarn**. Place the shoestring or yarn and the **Number Necklaces instruction card (page 95)** in the bag, and place the bag in the kit.

Kids in the News

Children will write answers to questions about their families.

Copy the **Kids in the News reproducible (page 96)** for each child, and place the papers in a **file folder**. Glue the **Kids in the News instruction card (page 95)** to the cover of the folder. Place the folder in the kit. When each child has completed this activity, bind the papers together in a class book titled *Kids in the News*.

Number of Sounds in Our Names

Children will identify the number of syllables in their class-mates' names.

Write *Number of Sounds in Our Names* on a **sentence strip half**. Tape the **Number of Sounds in Our Names instruction card (page 95)** to another sentence strip, and place it behind the first strip. Write the syllabicated name of each child (e.g., *Lind say*, *Al ex an der*) on separate sentence strip halves. Above each name, write the numbers 1, 2, 3, and 4. Laminate the strips. Place the name strips behind the instruction card strip. Hole-punch one end of each strip, and insert a **metal ring** through the hole to make a flip book. Clip a **transparency marker** to the flip book, and place the flip book in the kit.

Number Fun Notebook Instruction Cards

Materials
- lacing beads
- shoestring or piece of yarn

Number Necklaces
1. Find the bead with the smallest number, and slip it on the piece of string.
2. Choose the bead with the next largest number, and slip it on the string.
3. Repeat the activity until all the beads are on the string in order from smallest to largest.
4. Tie a knot at the end of the string
5. Place the string of beads in the bag, and return all items to the kit.

Materials
- folder

Kids in the News

My first name is _____
Our family's last name is _____
Our phone number is _____
Our home address is _____
We have _____ people in our home.
I have _____ brothers and _____ sisters.
My mom works at _____
My dad works at _____
We have _____ pets. Their names are _____

Our favorite thing to do together is _____

We took a family vacation to _____

Our favorite meal at home is _____
Our favorite place to eat out is _____
Our favorite song to sing together is _____
Our favorite book to read together is _____

Kids in the News
1. You will write a news report about your family.
2. Remove a paper from the folder.
3. Draw a picture of your family in the box at the top of the paper.
4. Answer the questions on the paper, and return it to the folder.
5. Return the folder to the kit.

Materials
- Number of Sounds in Our Names flip book
- transparency marker
- paper towel

Number of Sounds in Our Names
1. Open the flip book, and read each name you see.
2. Each name is made of one or more sounds called syllables.
3. Read each name again, and clap each time you hear a new sound or syllable. Count the number of times you clapped, and use the special marker to circle that number at the top of the card to show the number of syllables in the person's name.
4. Ask someone to check your work, and then use a damp paper towel to clean each "page" in the flip book.
5. Return the flip book to the kit.

Kids in the News

My first name is _____.

Our family's last name is _____.

Our phone number is _____.

Our home address is _____.

We have _____ people in our home.

I have _____ brothers and _____ sisters.

My mom works at _____.

My dad works at _____.

We have _____ pets. Their names are _____

_____.

Our favorite thing to do together is _____

_____.

We took a family vacation to _____

_____.

Our favorite meal at home is _____.

Our favorite place to eat out is _____.

Our favorite song to sing together is _____.

Our favorite book to read together is _____.

Literacy Bags © 2002 Creative Teaching Press

Our Outing to the Ocean

Use a fabric marker to write *Our Outing to the Ocean* on one side of a beach bag.

Alternative Theme Ideas

- Find fabric with an ocean, octopus, orange, ostrich, otter, or owl print, and use it to make a bag (see page 4).

- Use a fabric marker to write *Octopus' Overnight Bag* on the side of a duffel bag.

Literature Links

- *Commotion in the Ocean* by Giles Andreae (Orchard Books)
- *I Know An Old Lady Who Swallowed A Pie* by Alison Jackson (Dutton)
- *Kipper's Book of Opposites* by Mick Inkpen (Harcourt)
- *An Octopus Followed Me Home* by Dan Yaccarino (Puffin Books)
- *Oranges for Orange Juice* by Rozanne Lanczak Williams (Creative Teaching Press)

- *Out of the Ocean* by Debra Fraser (Harcourt)
- *Owl Babies* by Martin Waddell (Candlewick Press)
- *Owly* by Mike Thaler (Walker and Company)
- *There Was An Old Lady Who Swallowed a Fly* by Simms Taback (Viking)
- *The Underwater Alphabet Book* by Jerry Pallotta (Charlesbridge Publishing)

Playtime Props

★ octopus, ostrich, otter, or owl stuffed animals or puppets
★ old maid card game
★ Operation® game

Snacks to Sort, Sound Out, and Share

♥ oatmeal cookies
♥ Oreos®
♥ Ouch® bubble gum

Our Outing to the Ocean
Parent Journal

Please use this journal to record your comments or questions about the games and activities you have enjoyed with your child.

Literacy Bags © 2002 Creative Teaching Press

Our Outing to the Ocean
Student Journal

Here are some of the things you can write in this journal.

1. Read one of the books in the kit, and write about your favorite part of the story.

2. Write your own story.

3. Write about a trip to the ocean that you have taken or would like to take.

4. List as many words as you can that begin with the letter o.

5. Write about your favorite game or activity in this kit. Tell why you liked it.

Remember: Always write your name before you write anything else in the journal!

Literacy Bags © 2002 Creative Teaching Press

Our Outing to the Ocean Preparations

Ocean Memory Game

Children will practice memory skills and read new vocabulary words.

Copy the **Ocean Memory Game Cards (pages 101–102)** on **card stock**, cut them apart, and laminate them. Put the game cards and the **Ocean Memory Game instruction card (page 100)** in a **resealable bag**, and place the bag in the kit.

Our Overnight Book

Children will write about a personal experience.

Copy the **Our Overnight Book reproducible (page 103)** for each child, and place the papers in a **file folder**. Tape the **Our Overnight Book instruction card (page 100)** to the cover of the folder. Put **colored pencils** in a **resealable bag**, and place all items in the kit. When each child has completed this activity, bind the papers together in a class book titled *Our Overnight Book*.

Opposite Dominoes

Children will identify and match pairs of opposites.

Copy the **Opposite Dominoes reproducibles (pages 104–105)** on **card stock**, color them, cut them apart, and laminate them. Put the "dominoes" and the **Opposite Dominoes instruction card (page 100)** in a **resealable bag**, and place the bag in the kit.

Our Outing to the Ocean Instruction Cards

Materials
✐ Ocean Memory Game cards

Ocean Memory Game
1. Find someone to play this game with you.
2. Arrange the cards facedown in even rows on a flat surface.
3. Choose one person to go first. The first person turns over two cards. If the word on the card matches the picture, the person keeps the pair of cards and plays again until he or she turns over two cards that do not match.
4. The second person repeats the process.
5. Play until no cards remain.
6. Place the cards back in the bag, and return the bag to the kit.

Materials
✐ folder
✐ colored pencils

Our Overnight Book
1. Remove a paper from the folder.
2. Draw in the box a picture of you sleeping at another person's house.
3. Read the questions at the bottom of the page, and write your answers on the lines.
4. Place your paper back in the folder, place the colored pencils back in the bag, and return all items to the kit.

Materials
✐ bag of dominoes

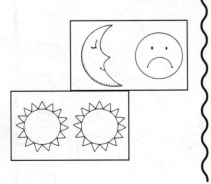

Opposite Dominoes
1. Find someone to play this game with you, and divide the dominoes between you and the other person.
2. The person who has the domino with two pictures that are the same places that domino on a flat surface.
3. The next person places a domino with an opposite picture beside one picture on the first domino.
4. Take turns placing dominoes with opposite pictures beside each other until no dominoes remain.
5. Place the dominoes back in the bag, and return the bag to the kit.

Ocean Memory Game Cards

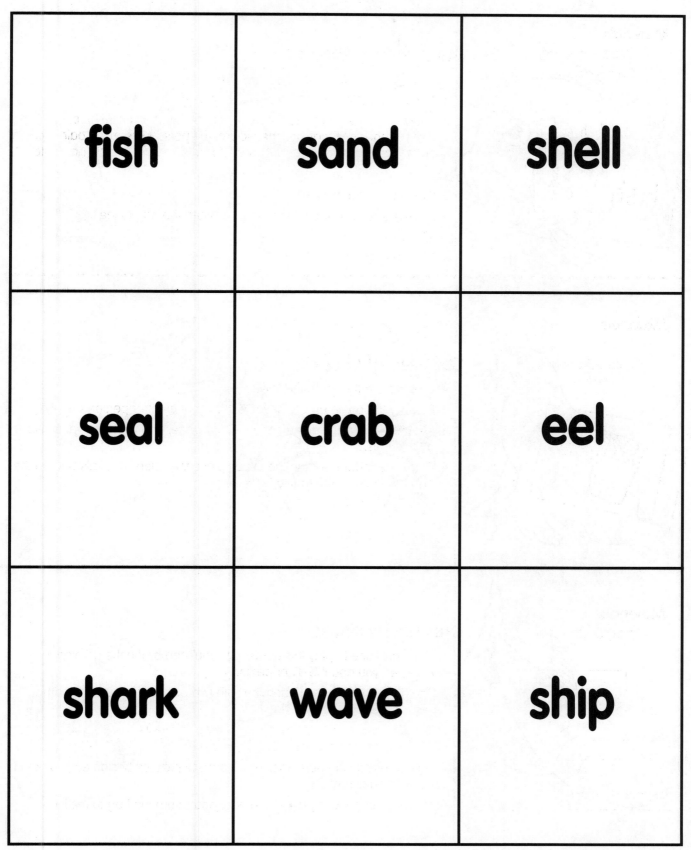

fish	sand	shell
seal	crab	eel
shark	wave	ship

Ocean Memory Game Cards

Our Overnight Book

At whose house are you sleeping?

_____

What did you take with you on your overnight trip?

_____

What did you do before you went to sleep?

_____

How did you feel on your overnight trip?

_____

Opposite Dominoes

Opposite Dominoes

Packing for a Picnic

Use a paint marker to write *Packing for a Picnic* on the side of a picnic basket.

Alternative Theme Ideas

- Find fabric with a pancake, parrot, peanut, pear, pelican, pencil/pen, penguin, pickle, pig, pocket, police officer, pony, popcorn, porcupine, potato, pumpkin, or puppy print, and use it to make a bag (see page 4).

- Find a large pail, and use a paint marker to write *Project Pail* on one side.

- Find a large clean pizza box, and use a paint marker to write *Pizza Playtime* on one side.

Literature Links

- ➡ *The Bear's Picnic* by Stan and Jan Berenstain (Random House)
- ➡ *Five Little Piggies* by David Martin (Candlewick Press)
- ➡ *Hold the Anchovies! A Book About Pizza* by Shelley Rotner (Orchard Books)
- ➡ *Pack a Picnic* by Kimberlee Graves (Creative Teaching Press)
- ➡ *Pancakes for Breakfast* by Tomie DePaola (Harcourt)

- ➡ *Pete's Pizza* by William Steig (HarperCollins)
- ➡ *Pigs* by Rozanne Lanczak Williams (Creative Teaching Press)
- ➡ *Polar Bear, Polar Bear What Do You Hear?* by Bill Martin Jr. (Henry Holt and Company)
- ➡ *Possum Magic* by Mem Fox (Harcourt)
- ➡ *Puffin's Climb, Penguin's Rhyme* by Bruce McMillan (Harcourt)

Playtime Props

- ★ parrot, pelican, penguin, pig, pony, porcupine, or puppy stuffed animals or puppets
- ★ pattern blocks
- ★ peg boards
- ★ pencils, pens, and/or paintbrushes
- ★ plastic peanuts, pears, pie, pizza, plums, popcorn, or pumpkins
- ★ Play-Doh®
- ★ Power Ranger® action figure
- ★ puzzles
- ★ toy piano

Snacks to Sort, Sound Out, and Share

- ♥ peanuts
- ♥ peppermints
- ♥ popcorn
- ♥ Poptarts®
- ♥ pretzels
- ♥ pudding

Packing for a Picnic
Student Journal

Here are some of the things you can write in this journal.

1. Read one of the books in the kit, and write about your favorite part of the story.

2. Write your own story.

3. Write about a picnic you have gone on.

4. List as many words as you can that begin with the letter p.

5. Write about your favorite game or activity in this kit. Tell why you liked it.

Remember: Always write your name before you write anything else in the journal!

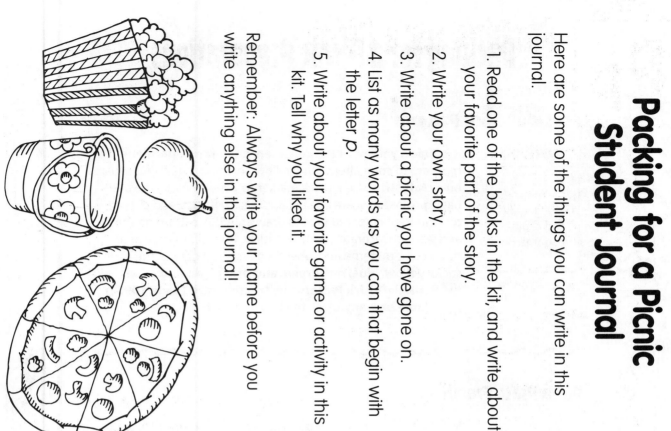

Packing for a Picnic
Parent Journal

Please use this journal to record your comments or questions about the games and activities you have enjoyed with your child.

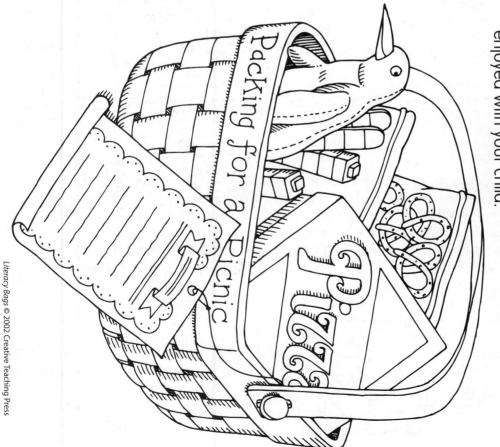

Packing for a Picnic Preparations

Popsicle®-Stick Patterns

Children will identify and copy patterns.

Use **black, yellow, blue, red, green, and orange permanent markers** to color alternating yellow and blue 1" (2.5 cm) squares on a **craft stick**. Use a black marker to write *ABAB* on the alternating colored squares. Select another craft stick, and choose two different color markers to draw an ABBA pattern on the stick and label it. Decorate additional sticks with different two- and three-color patterns, and label them accordingly. Put the craft sticks; **yellow, blue, red, green, and orange linking cubes**; and the **Popsicle®-Stick Patterns instruction card (page 109)** in a **resealable bag**, and place the bag in the kit.

Pizza Plate Fractions

Children will identify and manipulate fractional parts of an object.

Make four copies of the **Pizza reproducible (page 110)**, and color them. Cut one pizza in half, one in thirds, and one in fourths. Leave the last pizza intact. Laminate the pieces. Put all the pizza pieces and four **paper plates** in a **pizza box**. Glue the **Pizza Plate Fractions instruction card (page 109)** to the cover of the box, and place the box in the kit.

Pretzel Play

Children will sort pretzels by size and shape.

Copy the **Pretzel Play reproducible (page 111)** on **card stock** for each child, and place the papers in a **file folder**. Glue the **Pretzel Play instruction card (page 109)** to the cover of the folder, and laminate it. Put **assorted pretzels (e.g., rings, rods, sticks)** in a **resealable bag**, and place the bag and the folder in the kit.

Packing for a Picnic Instruction Cards

Materials
- patterned Popsicle® sticks
- linking cubes
- student journal

Popsicle®-Stick Patterns

1. Place the sticks on a flat surface.
2. Sort the cubes by color.
3. Select a stick. Use the linking cubes to build the pattern on the stick.
4. Select another stick, and use the linking cubes to build the pattern on it.
5. Repeat the activity until no sticks remain.
6. Choose your favorite pattern, and draw it in the student journal.
7. Use linking cubes to make your own pattern, and draw it in the journal.
8. Place the sticks and cubes back in the bag, and return all items to the kit.

Materials
- pizza box with pizza pieces and paper plates

Pizza Plate Fractions

1. Put the pizza pieces together to make four pizzas.
2. Use the paper plates to set the "table" for four people. Choose the pizza that is cut for four people, and place a piece of that pizza on each of the four plates.
3. Do the same thing with the pizzas that are cut for three and two people.
4. Invite another person or people to play "restaurant" with you. Practice dividing the pizzas so that everyone gets a fair share.
5. Place the pizza pieces and plates back in the box, and return the box to the kit.

Materials
- folder
- bag of pretzels

Pretzel Play

1. Remove a paper from the folder, and place it on a flat surface.
2. Remove ten pretzels from the bag, and place them at the top of the paper.
3. Ask someone to read the words on the paper to you, and use the pretzels to follow the directions.
4. Make patterns on the back of the paper with the rest of the pretzel pieces, and then eat them.
5. Return the folder to the kit.

Pizza

Literacy Bags © 2002 Creative Teaching Press

Pretzel Play

I have ten pretzel pieces in all shapes and sizes.
Follow along for some pretzel surprises.

I can make a picture and a pattern, too.

I can even make them disappear for you.
Line them up below, side-by-side, one-by-one.
I'll eat them by twos until there are none.

Ten crunchy pretzels sit on my plate.
I will eat two, and now there are eight.

Eight crunchy pretzel rods, rings, and sticks.
I will eat two, and now there are six.

Six crunchy pretzels that I bought at the store.
I will eat two, and now there are four.

Four crunchy pretzels are so much fun to chew.
I will eat two, and now there are two.

Two crunchy pretzels—their taste can't be outdone.
I will eat two, and now there are none!

Queen's Quilt Bag

Find an old quilt, and use it to make a bag (see page 4). Use a fabric marker to write *Queen's Quilt Bag* on one side of the bag.

Alternative Theme Ideas

- Find fabric with a quacking duck, quail, quarter, or queen print, and use it to make a bag (see page 4).

- Cover a box with paper, and draw webbed footprints in a path around it. Draw drops of water around the footprints. Use a paint marker to write *How Do You Catch a Quick Quackeroo?* on one side.

Literature Links

- ➥ *The Log Cabin Quilt* by Ellen Howard (Holiday House)
- ➥ *No Tooth, No Quarter* by Jon Buller and Susan Schade (Random House)
- ➥ *Quack and Count* by Keith Baker (Harcourt)
- ➥ *Quack: The Sound of Q* by Cynthia F. Klingel and Robert B. Noyed (Child's World)
- ➥ *Quacky Duck* by Paul Rogers (Little, Brown, and Company)
- ➥ *Quacky Quack-Quack!* by Ian Whybrow (Four Winds Press)
- ➥ *Quilt of Dreams* by Mindy Dwyer (Alaska Northwest Books)
- ➥ *The Quilt Story* by Tony Johnston (Putnam)
- ➥ *Selina and the Bear Paw Quilt* by Barbara Smucker (Dragonflyer Press)
- ➥ *The Very Quiet Cricket* by Eric Carle (Philomel)

Playtime Props
★ duck or quail stuffed animals or puppets
★ crown
★ queen figurine or puppet

Snacks to Sort, Sound Out, and Share
♥ Quaker® Squares cereal
♥ Suzy Q's®

Queen's Quilt Bag
Student Journal

Here are some of the things you can write in this journal.

1. Read one of the books in the kit, and write about your favorite part of the story.

2. Write your own story.

3. Write about what you think a queen does.

4. List as many words as you can that begin with the letter q.

5. Write about your favorite game or activity in this kit. Tell why you liked it.

Remember: Always write your name before you write anything else in the journal!

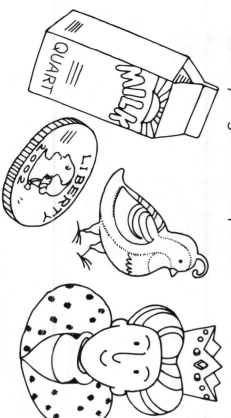

- -

Queen's Quilt Bag
Parent Journal

Please use this journal to record your comments or questions about the games and activities you have enjoyed with your child.

Queen's Quilt Bag Preparations

Quilt Creations

Children will make patterns with various geometric shapes.

Copy the **Quilt Square reproducible (page 116)** on **card stock**. (As an option, color the shapes on the quilt square to match the colors of the same shape pattern blocks.) Laminate the paper. Copy the Quilt Square reproducible for each child, and place the papers in a **file folder**. Glue the **Quilt Creations instruction card (page 115)** to the cover of the folder. Put a set of **pattern blocks** in a **resealable bag**, and place all items in the kit. When each child has completed this activity, tape the papers together to create a class "quilt."

Quarters for a Queen

Children will practice manipulating quarters.

Copy the **Quarters for a Queen reproducible (page 117)** on **card stock**, color it, and laminate it. Put **quarters** and the **Quarters for a Queen instruction card (page 115)** in a **resealable bag**, and place all items in the kit.

Locating the Queen's Quacker

Children will practice giving and following oral directions.

Put a **rubber or stuffed duck** and the **Locating the Queen's Quacker instruction card (page 115)** in a **resealable bag**, and place the bag in the kit.

Queen's Quilt Bag Instruction Cards

Materials
- laminated Quilt Square paper
- folder
- pattern blocks
- crayons

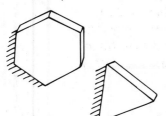

Quilt Creations

1. Place the laminated Quilt Square paper on a flat surface.
2. Sort the pattern blocks by shape.
3. Place the pattern blocks over the matching shapes on the paper.
4. Place the pattern blocks back in the bag, and remove a paper from the folder.
5. Use crayons to color your own pattern on the square.
6. Place your paper back in the folder, and return all items to the kit.

Materials
- Quarters for a Queen paper
- quarters

Quarters for a Queen

1. Place the correct number of quarters near each item the queen would like to buy.
2. Place the quarters back in the bag, and return all items to the kit.

Materials
- duck

Locating the Queen's Quacker

1. Ask someone to play this game with you.
2. Close your eyes, and ask the other person to hide the duck.
3. Ask the person who hid the duck yes or no questions to help you find it. For example, ask *Is it up high*? or *Is it inside something else*?
4. When you think you know where you can find the duck, say *Quack, quack!*, and tell the person where you think the duck is.
5. When you find the duck, switch roles with the other person, and play again.
6. Return the duck to the kit.

Quilt Square

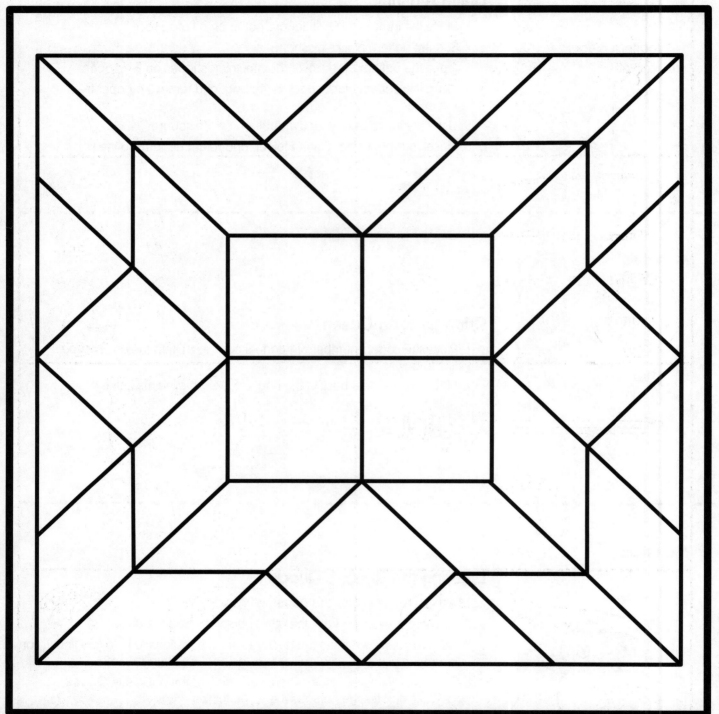

Literacy Bags © 2002 Creative Teaching Press

Quarters for a Queen

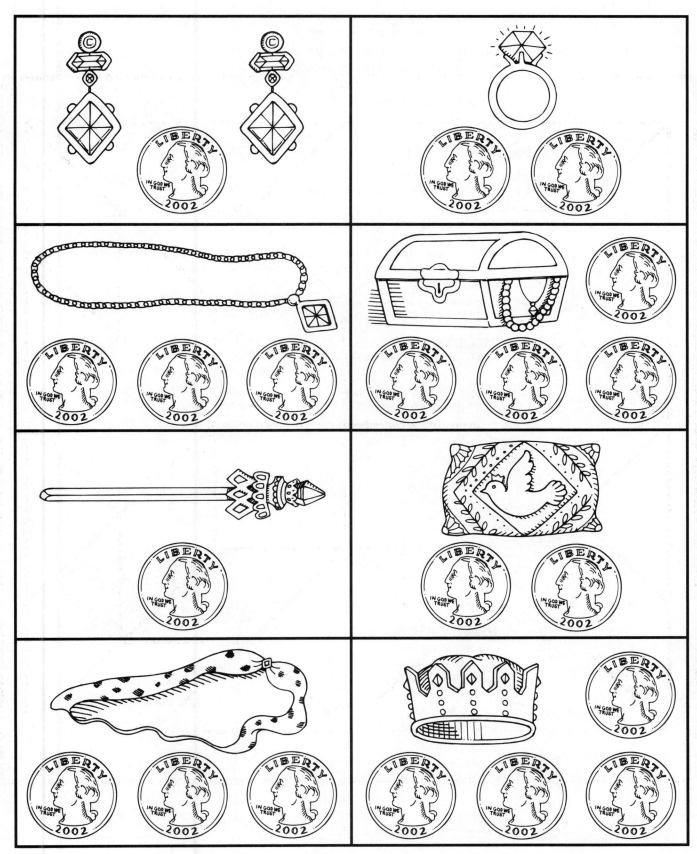

Reading Rodeo

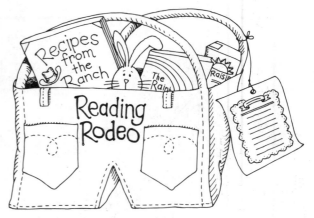

Find an old pair of denim jeans. Cut off the legs, and stitch together both openings. Use the denim from the legs or a bandana to make handles, and sew them to the top of the bag near the belt loops. Use a fabric pen to write *Reading Rodeo* across one side of the bag.

Alternative Theme Ideas

- Find fabric with a rabbit, raccoon, railroad, rain, rainbow, rectangle, reindeer, reptile, rhinoceros, robin, robot, rocket, rose, or rowboat print, and use it to make a bag (see page 4).

- Find a large white bucket. Glue white felt ears, large wiggly eyes, a pink pom-pom nose, black pipe cleaner whiskers, and a white pom-pom tail to the bucket. Use a paint marker to write *Our Reading Rabbit* on one side.

Literature Links

- *Armadillo Rodeo* by Jan Brett (Putnam's Sons)
- *Blue Rabbit and Friends* by Christopher Wormell (Phyllis Fogelman Books)
- *I Love You, Bunny Rabbit* by Shulamith Oppenheim (Boyds Mills Press)
- *The Little Red Hen* by Byron Barton (HarperCollins)
- *Mr. Noisy at the Dude Ranch* by Margaret Allen (Creative Teaching Press)
- *My River* by Shari Halpern (Macmillan)
- *Raccoon on His Own* by Jim Arnosky (Putnam's Sons)
- *Rainbow Fish* by Marcus Pfister (North-South Books)
- *Rosie's Walk* by Pat Hutchins (Aladdin)
- *Yippee-Yay: A Book about Cowboys and Cowgirls* by Gail Gibbons (Holiday House)

Playtime Props

★ rabbit, raccoon, reindeer, reptile, rhinoceros, or robin stuffed animals or puppets
★ rabbit ear headband
★ rings
★ Rubic's® Cube
★ Rummy-O®

Snacks to Sort, Sound Out, and Share

♥ raisins
♥ ring pops
♥ Rollos®

Reading Rodeo
Student Journal

Here are some of the things you can write in this journal.

1. Read one of the books in the kit, and write about your favorite part of the story.

2. Write your own story.

3. Imagine that you live on a ranch. Write about your life.

4. List as many words as you can that begin with the letter r.

5. Write about your favorite game or activity in this kit. Tell why you liked it.

Remember: Always write your name before you write anything else in the journal!

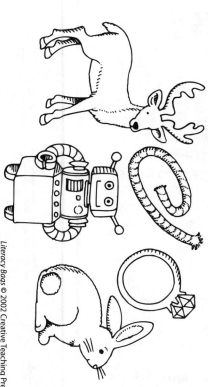

Reading Rodeo
Parent Journal

Please use this journal to record your comments or questions about the games and activities you have enjoyed with your child.

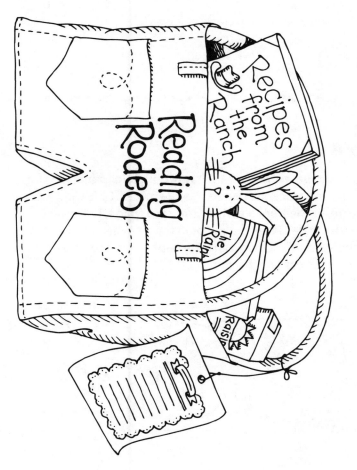

Reading Rodeo Preparations

Race to the Rodeo

Children will solve simple addition problems.

Copy the **Race to the Rodeo Game Board (page 122)**, and color it. Open a **file folder**, and glue the paper to one side. Glue the **Race to the Rodeo instruction card (page 121)** to the cover of the folder, and laminate it. Copy the **Race to the Rodeo Game Cards (page 123)** on **card stock**, laminate them, and cut them apart. Put the cards in a **resealable bag**. Attach a different **sticker** to four separate **pennies**, and put them in the bag. Place all items in the kit.

Rodeo Rhyming

Children will identify and spell rhyming words.

Copy the **Rodeo Rhyming Cards (page 124)** on **card stock**, laminate them, and cut them apart. Attach a piece of **magnetic tape** to the back of each card. Put the rhyming cards, a set of **magnetic letters**, and the **Rodeo Rhyming instruction card (page 121)** in a **resealable bag**, and place the bag in the kit.

Recipes from the Ranch

Children will write a recipe.

Copy the **Recipe from the Ranch reproducible (page 125)** for each child, and place the papers in a **file folder**. Glue the **Recipes from the Ranch instruction card (page 121)** to the cover of the folder. Place the folder in the kit. When each child has completed this activity, bind the papers together in a class book titled *Recipes from the Ranch*.

Reading Rodeo Instruction Cards

Materials
- Race to the Rodeo game board
- Race to the Rodeo game cards
- game markers

Race to the Rodeo

1. Find one, two, or three other people to play this game with you. Place the game board on a flat surface.
2. Each person takes a different penny (game marker) and places it near "Start" on the board.
3. Shuffle the cards into a pile, and place it facedown.
4. One player draws a card, answers the addition problem, and moves his or her game marker the same number of spaces as the answer.
5. The next player repeats the activity.
6. Repeat until all players cross the finish line.
7. Place the cards and game markers back in the bag, and return all items to the kit.

Materials
- Rodeo Rhyming cards
- magnetic letters
- magnetic surface (e.g., refrigerator, cookie sheet)

Rodeo Rhyming

1. Place the cards on a magnetic surface.
2. Arrange the cards so that the rhyming words are beside each other.
3. Use magnetic letters to spell the word on each card. Place the magnetic letters directly below the letters printed on the card.
4. Ask someone to check your work.
5. Place the cards and letters back in the bag, and return all items to the kit.

Materials
- folder
- crayons or markers

Recipes from the Ranch

1. Remove a paper from the folder. Write your name at the top of the paper.
2. Think of a food you like to eat, and write it on the next line of the paper.
3. Draw a picture of this food in the space provided.
4. Make a list of the things you need to make this food or dish.
5. Tell how you put everything together to make the dish.
6. Place your paper back in the folder, and return the folder to the kit.

Race to the Rodeo Game Board

Race to the Rodeo Game Cards

3+0	0+2	1+0	0+1
4+0	0+3	1+1	1+1
0+0	0+4	1+2	2+1
2+2	2+0	1+3	3+1

Rodeo Rhyming Cards

bag

hat

gate

flag

cat

date

star

man

ride

far

can

hide

Literacy Bags © 2002 Creative Teaching Press

Recipe from the Ranch

by _____

This is a recipe for _____.

This is how it looks.

These are the ingredients you will need:

_____   _____

_____   _____

_____   _____

These are the directions for making this recipe:

_____

_____

_____

_____

_____

_____

_____

Literacy Bags © 2002 Creative Teaching Press

Ss

Science Sack

Turn a plain pillowcase inside out. At the opening at the top, cut two small slits side by side through one layer of the fabric. Put a light rope or heavy string through one slit. Thread it through the top of the pillowcase and out the second slit. Loosely tie together the ends of the rope or string. Use fabric paint to decorate the pillowcase with pictures of test tubes, balances, and other scientific equipment, and use a fabric pen to write *Science Sack* on one side.

Alternative Theme Ideas

- Find fabric with a sailboat, sandwich, scarecrow, school, sea, seal, shark, sheep, shoe, skating, skunk, snail, snake, soccer, sock, space, spider, summer, sun, or sunglasses print, and use it to make a bag (see page 4).

- Cover a box with dark contact paper. Attach glittery or glow-in-the-dark star stickers to the box. Use a paint marker to write *I Spy Stars in the Sky* on one side.

- Find a shoe box, and use a marker to write *Shoe Box Schoolwork* on one side.

Literature Links

- *Big Silver Space Shuttle* by Ken Wilson-Max (David Bennett Books)
- *Draw Me a Star* by Eric Carle (Philomel)
- *Hide and Snake* by Keith Baker (Harcourt)
- *I Spy* by Margaret Allen (Creative Teaching Press)
- *Our Stars* by Anne Rockwell (Harcourt)
- *A Pair of Socks* by Stuart J. Murphy (HarperCollins)
- *Silly Sally* by Audrey Wood (Harcourt)
- *Some Smug Slug* by Pamela Duncan Edwards (HarperCollins)
- *Stellaluna* by Janell Cannon (Harcourt)
- *Twinkle, Twinkle, Little Star* by Iza Trapani (Whispering Coyote)

Playtime Props

★ sailor hat
★ seal, shark, sheep, skunk, snail, snake, or spider stuffed animals or puppets
★ Silly Putty®
★ Skip-Bo Jr.® card game
★ Spirograph®
★ spoons
★ sun visor
★ sunglasses

Snacks to Sort, Sound Out, and Share

♥ Skittles®
♥ strawberry candy
♥ suckers
♥ sunflower seeds
♥ Sweet Tarts®

Science Sack
Student Journal

Here are some of the things you can write in this journal.

1. Read one of the books in the kit, and write about your favorite part of the story.

2. Write your own story.

3. Imagine that you are a scientist and you discover something new. Write about it.

4. List as many words as you can that begin with the letter s.

5. Write about your favorite game or activity in this kit. Tell why you liked it.

Remember: Always write your name before you write anything else in the journal!

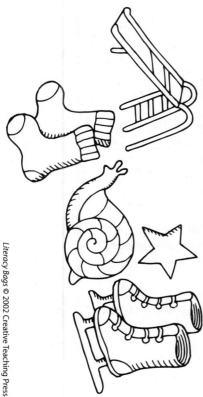

Science Sack
Parent Journal

Please use this journal to record your comments or questions about the games and activities you have enjoyed with your child.

Science Sack Preparations

Solar System Science

Children will identify the planets and learn their names.

Copy the **Our Solar System reproducible (page 130)** on **card stock**, and color the planets. Cut apart the cards. Open a **file folder**, and glue the cards in the following order: Mercury, Venus, Earth, Mars, Jupiter, Saturn, Uranus, Neptune, and Pluto. Glue the **Solar System Science instruction card (page 129)** to the cover of the folder, and laminate it. Make another copy of the Our Solar System reproducible, and color the planets. Cut out the planets only, laminate them, and put them and a set of **colored pencils** in a **resealable bag**. Place the bag, **books about the solar system**, and the folder in the kit.

Simple Science Experiment

Children will explore colors and record their observations.

Put **coffee filters**, **markers**, **cups**, and the **Simple Science Experiment instruction card (page 129)** in a **resealable bag**, and place the bag in the kit.

Stellar Sorting

Children will count, divide, and then sort stars by color, size, and design.

Make several copies of the **Stars reproducible (page 131)** on **card stock**, and cut out the stars. Use **art supplies (e.g., gel pens, glitter, glue, markers, sequins)** to decorate the stars in ways that children can sort them into groups (e.g., color the patterns on two different small stars green or put red glitter on one small star and one large star), and then laminate them. Put the stars and the **Stellar Sorting instruction card (page 129)** in a **resealable bag**, and place the bag in the kit.

Science Sack Instruction Cards

Materials
- folder
- planet cutouts
- books about the solar system
- colored pencils
- student journal

Solar System Science

1. Match the planet cutouts with the planets in the folder. Ask someone to help you read the names of the planets.
2. Look for the planets in the books about the solar system.
3. Draw one or more of the planets in the student journal, and write about what you learned about this planet in a book.
4. Place the planet cutouts, colored pencils, and books back in the bag, and return all items to the kit.

Materials
- coffee filters
- markers
- cups
- student journal

Simple Science Experiment

1. Remove a coffee filter, a cup, and the markers from the bag.
2. Fold the coffee filter in half. Keep folding it in half again until it has the shape of a thin triangle.
3. Use the markers to color a pattern on both sides of the filter.
4. Fill the cup with a little water, and dip the pointed end of the filter in it.
5. Wait for 5 minutes.
6. Remove the filter from the cup, and unfold it.
7. Allow the filter to dry while you write in the student journal what you think happened to the colors on the filter.
8. Keep your coffee filter, but return all other items to the kit.

Materials
- stars

Stellar Sorting

1. Place the stars on a flat surface.
2. Count how many stars there are.
3. Divide the stars into two groups. How many stars are there in each group? Are there any left over?
4. Divide the stars into three groups. How many stars are there in each group? Are there any left over?
5. Sort the stars into different groups.
6. Place the stars back in the bag, and return it to the kit.

Our Solar System

Mercury

Venus

Earth

Mars

Jupiter

Saturn

Uranus

Neptune

Pluto

Stars

Teddy Bear's Toolbox

Use a paint marker to write *Teddy Bear's Toolbox* on one side of a toolbox. Attach stickers of tools and teddy bears to the sides.

Alternative Theme Ideas

- Find fabric with a teddy bear, teeth, telephone, tiger, toad, tool, tractor, train, treasure, tree, triangle, tricycle, tornado, toy, trombone, truck, trumpet, tuba, turkey, or turtle print, and use it to make a bag (see page 4).

- Paint orange and black stripes on a plain canvas bag. Braid together several strands of orange and black yarn, and use a hot glue gun to attach it to the bag to create a "tail." Use fabric paint to write *Tiger's Tall Tales* on one side.

Literature Links

- *How a House Is Built* by Gail Gibbons (Holiday House)
- *Little Green Tow Truck* by Ken Wilson-Max (David Bennett Books)
- *Teddy Bear for Sale* by Gail Herman (Scholastic)
- *The Teddy Bears Picnic* by Jimmy Kennedy (Henry Holt and Company)
- *Telling Time with Big Mama Cat* by Dan Harper (Harcourt)
- *Truck* by Donald Crews (Greenwillow Books)
- *Truck Tricks* by Margaret Allen (Creative Teaching Press)
- *Turtle Splash! Countdown at the Pond* by Cathryn Falwell (Greenwillow Books)
- *Two Greedy Bears* by Mirra Ginsburg (Aladdin)
- *Where's My Teddy?* by Jez Alborough (Candlewick Press)

Playtime Props

★ spinning top
★ tape player
★ teddy bear, tiger, turkey, or turtle stuffed animals or puppets
★ telephone
★ tic-tac-toe
★ toys
★ tractor
★ train
★ treasure chest
★ truck
★ Tyrannosaurus rex toy figure

Snacks to Sort, Sound Out, and Share

♥ taffy
♥ Tootsie Rolls®
♥ Triscuits®
♥ Trix® cereal
♥ Twizzlers®

Teddy Bear's Toolbox
Student Journal

Here are some of the things you can write in this journal.

1. Read one of the books in the kit, and write about your favorite part of the story.

2. Write your own story.

3. Write about a time you fixed something.

4. List as many words as you can that begin with the letter *t*.

5. Write about your favorite game or activity in this kit. Tell why you liked it.

Remember: Always write your name before you write anything else in the journal!

- -

Teddy Bear's Toolbox
Parent Journal

Please use this journal to record your comments or questions about the games and activities you have enjoyed with your child.

Teddy Bear's Toolbox Preparations

Compare These Teddy Bears

Children will compare two objects and write about the differences.

Copy the **Compare These Teddy Bears reproducible (page 136)** for each child, and place the papers in a **file folder**. Glue the **Compare These Teddy Bears instruction card (page 135)** to the cover of the folder. Place the folder and **two different teddy bears** in the kit.

Telling Time with Teddy Bear

Children will practice telling time to the hour on an analog and a digital clock.

Copy the **Clocks reproducible (page 137)** on **card stock**, and laminate it. Cut out the clock face and the minute and hour hands. Cut small slits through the center of the clock face and at the ends of each hand, and use a **brass fastener** to attach the hands to the clock. Cut out the digital clock and number strip. Cut along the top and bottom lines of the first box on the digital clock, and slip the number strip through so that only one number shows at a time. Copy the **Time Cards (page 138)** on **card stock**, cut apart the cards, and laminate them. Put both clocks, the time cards, and the **Telling Time with Teddy Bear instruction card (page 135)** in a **resealable bag**, and place the bag in the kit.

Tangram Tile House

Children will follow directions to arrange tangram tiles.

Put **tangram tiles (2 large triangles, 1 medium triangle, 2 small triangles, 2 small squares, 1 small parallelogram)** and the **Tangram Tile House instruction card (page 135)** in a **resealable bag**, and place the bag in the kit.

Teddy Bear's Toolbox Instruction Cards

Materials
- folder
- teddy bears
- crayons or markers

Compare These Teddy Bears

1. Examine both teddy bears.
2. Remove a paper from the folder, and draw one teddy bear in each box.
3. Think about what is the same and what is different about the teddy bears, and answer the questions on your paper.
4. Place your paper back in the folder, and return all items to the kit.

Materials
- 2 clocks
- time cards

Telling Time with Teddy Bear

1. Practice changing the times on each clock.
2. Separate the time cards into two piles: one with words and one with numbers.
3. Select a time card from either pile, and show the time on the card on both clocks.
4. Ask someone to check your work.
5. Repeat the activity with a new time card.
6. After you have practiced setting the clocks, try to match the word time cards with the number time cards.
7. Place the clocks and cards back in the bag, and return the bag to the kit.

Materials
- tangram tiles

Tangram Tile House

1. Use the tangram tiles to build houses for teddy bear.
2. Make a large square with two tiles.
3. Make a small square with two tiles.
4. Make a house with two tiles.
5. Make a house with three tiles.
6. Make a rectangle with three tiles.
7. Make your own design with all eight tiles.
8. Place the tangram tiles back in the bag, and return the bag to the kit.

Compare These Teddy Bears

Bear 1   ## Bear 2

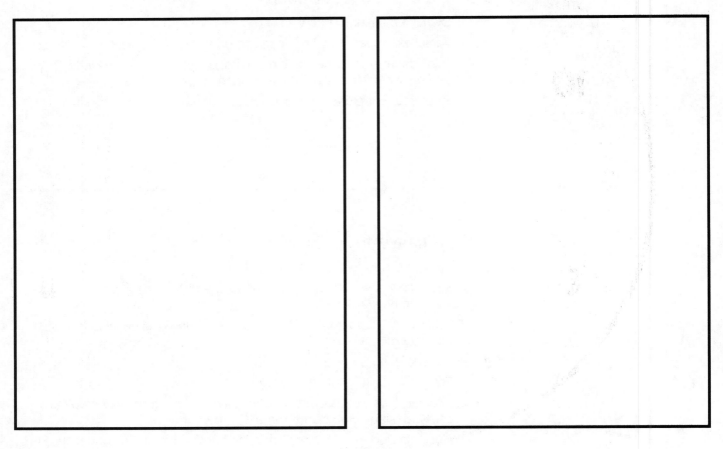

Which bear is bigger?	Bear 1	Bear 2
Which bear has bigger eyes?	Bear 1	Bear 2
Which bear is softer?	Bear 1	Bear 2
Which bear is wearing clothes?	Bear 1	Bear 2
Which bear would you like to hug?	Bear 1	Bear 2

Clocks

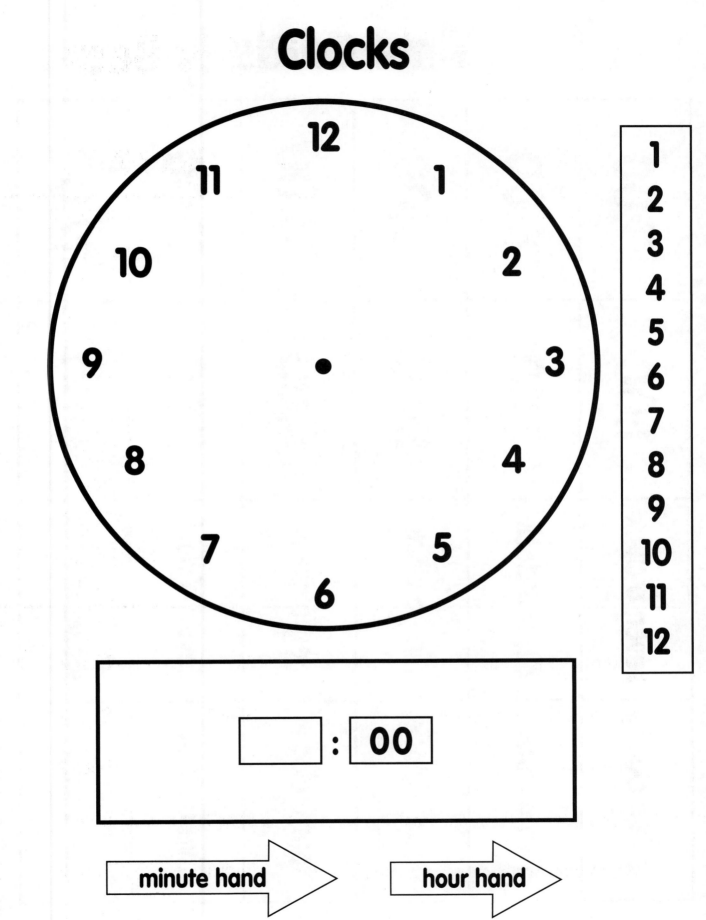

minute hand

hour hand

Literacy Bags © 2002 Creative Teaching Press

Time Cards

7:00	1:00	seven o'clock	one o'clock
8:00	2:00	eight o'clock	two o'clock
9:00	3:00	nine o'clock	three o'clock
10:00	4:00	ten o'clock	four o'clock
11:00	5:00	eleven o'clock	five o'clock
12:00	6:00	twelve o'clock	six o'clock

Literacy Bags © 2002 Creative Teaching Press

Uncle Sam's U.S.A. Bag

Use a paint marker to write *Uncle Sam's U.S.A. Bag* on a red, white, and blue gift bag. Tie red, white, and blue ribbon to the handles of the bag.

Alternative Theme Ideas

- Find fabric with a ukulele, umpire, unicorn, umbrella, Uncle Sam, or United States of America print, and use it to make a bag (see page 4).

- Use vinyl to make a bag (see page 4). Use a fabric marker to write *Our Unbelievable Umbrella Bag* on one side.

- Use paint markers to draw balloons on a canvas bag. Use a fabric marker to write *Up, Up and Away* on one side.

Literature Links

- *Beneath a Blue Umbrella* by Jack Prelutsky (Greenwillow Books)
- *The Flag of the United States* by Dennis B. Fradin (Children's Press)
- *The Fourth of July* by Janet McDonnell (Children's Press)
- *My Red Umbrella* by Robert Bright (William Morrow & Company)
- *Roger's Umbrella* by Daniel Pinkwater (Dutton)
- *The Ugly Duckling* by Bernadette Watts (North-South Books)
- *Umbrella* by Taro Yashima (Viking)
- *The Umbrella Day* by Nancy Evans Cooney (Philomel)
- *Umbrella Parade* by Kathy Feczko (Troll)
- *Up, Up, Down* by Robert Munsch (Scholastic)

Playtime Props

★ cocktail umbrellas
★ Uncle Sam doll
★ unicorn stuffed animal or puppet
★ Uno (My First)® card game
★ U.S.A. flag
★ U.S.A. puzzle

Snacks to Sort, Sound Out, and Share

♥ Nutter Butter® cookies
♥ blueberries
♥ unsalted crackers

Uncle Sam's U.S.A. Bag
Parent Journal

Please use this journal to record your comments or questions about the games and activities you have enjoyed with your child.

Uncle Sam's U.S.A. Bag
Student Journal

Here are some of the things you can write in this journal.

1. Read one of the books in the kit, and write about your favorite part of the story.

2. Write your own story.

3. Write about why you like living in the United States of America.

4. List as many words as you can that begin with the letter *u*.

5. Write about your favorite game or activity in this kit. Tell why you liked it.

Remember: Always write your name before you write anything else in the journal!

Uncle Sam's U.S.A. Bag Preparations

Where Are You in the U.S.A.?

Children will identify their state and its border states and read cardinal directions on a compass rose.

Make an enlarged copy of the **U.S. Map (page 143)**. Trace your state and the states that border it on **card stock**, and cut them out. Laminate the map and the state cutouts. Attach a piece of **Velcro** to the back of the state cutouts and to the same states on the map. Attach a piece of Velcro on all four sides of the map. Write *north, east, south,* and *west* on separate **index cards**, laminate them, and attach Velcro to the back of each card. Put the direction cards, the state cutouts, and the **Where Are You in the U.S.A.? instruction card (page 142)** in a **resealable bag**. Place the bag and the map in the kit.

Uppercase/Lowercase Match

Children will match uppercase and lowercase letters.

Put a set of **uppercase and lowercase magnetic letters** and the **Uppercase/Lowercase Match instruction card (page 142)** in a **resealable bag**, and place the bag in the kit.

Unscramble the Sentences

Children will arrange words into complete sentences.

Write four different simple sentences (e.g., *She is my friend.*) on **four different color sentence strips**, and laminate them. Cut apart the words on each strip, put the word cards and the **Unscramble the Sentences instruction card (page 142)** in a **resealable bag**, and place the bag in the kit.

Uncle Sam's U.S.A. Bag Instruction Cards

Materials

- map of the U.S.
- state cutouts
- direction cards

Where Are You in the U.S.A.?

1. Place the map on a flat surface.
2. Find your state in the pile of state cutouts, and attach it to the correct place on the map.
3. Attach the rest of the states to the correct places on the map.
4. Look at the compass rose at the bottom of the map, and use it to help you determine where to place the four direction cards.
5. Place the state cutouts and direction cards back in the bag, and return all items to the kit.

Materials

- magnetic letters
- magnetic surface (e.g., refrigerator, cookie sheet)

Uppercase/Lowercase Match

1. Place the letters on a magnetic surface, and match the uppercase and lowercase letters.
2. Place the letters back in the bag, and return the bag to the kit.

Materials

- word cards

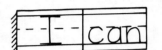

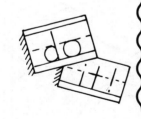

Unscramble the Sentences

1. Sort the cards by color.
2. Select one color of cards, and read the words you see.
3. Arrange the words to make a complete sentence.
4. Repeat the activity with the other cards to make three more sentences.
5. Place the cards back in the bag, and return the bag to the kit.

Literacy Bags © 2002 Creative Teaching Press

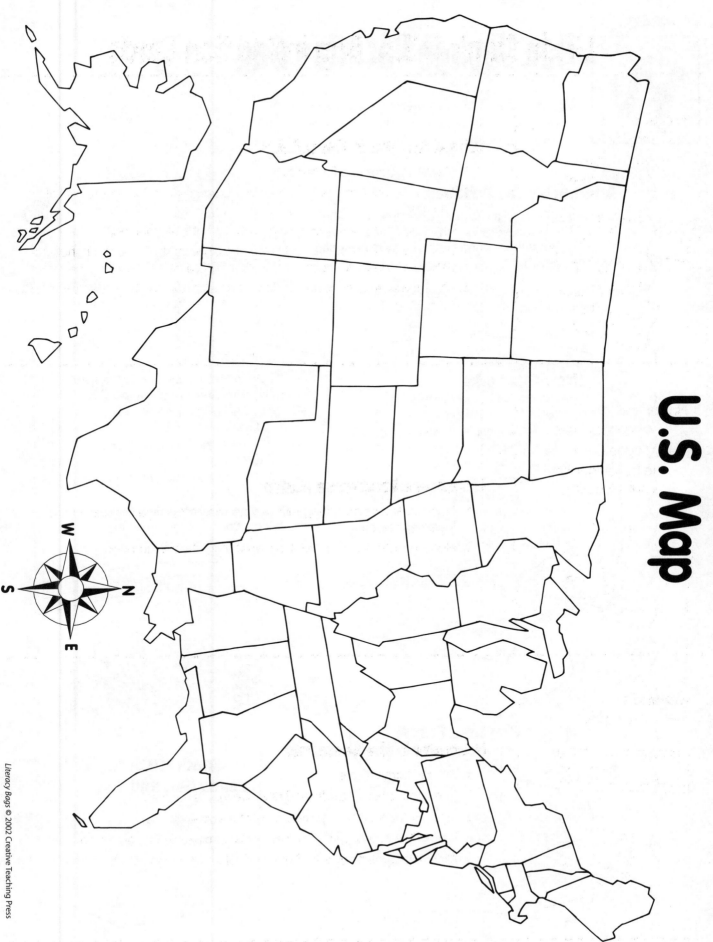

U.S. Map

Bon Voyage Vacation Bag

Use a fabric marker to write *Bon Voyage Vacation Bag* on one side of a suitcase that has wheels and a retractable handle.

Alternative Theme Ideas

- Find fabric with a vacation, valentine, vegetable, vehicle, Venus, veterinarian, video, volcano, volleyball, or vulture print, and use it to make a bag (see page 4).

- Use velvet or a violet-colored fabric to make a bag (see page 4).

Literature Links

- ➡ *Arthur's Family Vacation* by Marc Brown (Little, Brown and Company)
- ➡ *Eating the Alphabet: Fruits and Vegetables from A to Z* by Lois Ehlert (Harcourt)
- ➡ *Growing Vegetable Soup* by Lois Ehlert (Harcourt)
- ➡ *How I Spent My Summer Vacation* by Mark Teague (Crown)
- ➡ *Miss Violet's Shining Day* by Jane Breskin Zalben (Boyds Mills Press)
- ➡ *The Vegetable Show* by Laurene Krasney Brown (Little, Brown and Company)
- ➡ *The Very Hungry Caterpillar* by Eric Carle (Philomel)
- ➡ *The Very Noisy Night* by Diana Hendry (Dutton)
- ➡ *A Very Special House* by Ruth Krauss (Harper & Row)
- ➡ *The Victory Garden Vegetable Book* by Jerry Pallotta (Charlesbridge Publishing)

Playtime Props

★ plastic vegetables
★ vacation brochures
★ videos
★ volleyball
★ toy vans or other vehicles

Snacks to Sort, Sound Out, and Share

♥ V-8®
♥ vegetable crackers
♥ Velveeta® cheese

Bon Voyage Vacation Bag
Student Journal

Here are some of the things you can write in this journal.

1. Read one of the books in the kit, and write about your favorite part of the story.

2. Write your own story.

3. Write about a vacation you have taken or would like to take.

4. List as many words as you can that begin with the letter v.

5. Write about your favorite game or activity in this kit. Tell why you liked it.

Remember: Always write your name before you write anything else in the journal!

Bon Voyage Vacation Bag
Parent Journal

Please use this journal to record your comments or questions about the games and activities you have enjoyed with your child.

Bon Voyage Vacation Bag Preparations

Vacation Postcards

Children will write a message on a postcard.

Put the **Vacation Postcards instruction card (page 147)**, **index cards**, and **stickers (optional)** in a **resealable bag**. Place the bag in the kit.

Video of Vocabulary Words

Children will identify words that begin with the letter *v*.

Copy the **Television reproducible (page 148)** and the **Video of Vocabulary Words reproducible (page 149)** on **card stock**, color the pictures, and laminate the reproducibles. Cut out the two picture strips, and tape them together to create one strip. Cut out the television, and carefully cut along the two boldface lines. Put the strip through the slits so that only one illustration shows at a time. Put the television and the **Video of Vocabulary Words instruction card (page 147)** in a **resealable bag**, and place the bag in the kit.

Valentine Addition

Children will add quantities to ten.

Make two copies of the **Hearts reproducible (page 58)** on **red paper**, cut out the hearts, and laminate them. Glue the **Valentine Addition instruction card (page 147)** and two hearts to the cover of a **file folder**. Open the folder, and attach five pieces of **Velcro** to each side. Attach a piece of Velcro to the rest of the ten heart cutouts, and put them in a **resealable bag**. Make three copies of the **Valentine Addition reproducible (page 150)**. Write a number less than six in the first two hearts of each strip, and leave the third heart blank. Laminate the papers, and cut apart the strips. Put the strips and a **transparency marker** in the bag. Place the bag and the folder in the kit.

Bon Voyage Vacation Bag Instruction Cards

Materials
- index card
- crayons or colored pencils

Vacation Postcards

1. Draw a picture of a place that you have visited or would like to visit on one side of an index card.
2. Turn over the card. On the left side, write a short message to someone about this place, and sign your name. On the right side, write this person's address. Add a sticker to the top right corner for a stamp or draw your own.
3. Return all items to the kit.

Materials
- television cutout
- student journal

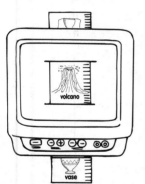

Video of Vocabulary Words

1. Slowly slide the strip through the "television."
2. Name what you see in each picture.
3. After you name each picture, return to the one you like the best, and write about this picture in the student journal.
4. Return all items to the kit.

Materials
- folder
- Valentine Addition strips
- heart cutouts
- transparency marker
- paper towel

Valentine Addition

1. Open the folder, and place it on a flat surface. Select a strip, and place it below the folder.
2. Look at the first number on the strip, and place that number of hearts on the left side of the folder.
3. Look at the second number on the strip, and place that number of hearts on the right side of the folder.
4. Count the number of hearts you see in all. Use the special marker to write the total number of hearts in the blank heart on the strip.
5. Repeat the activity with the rest of the eleven strips, and ask someone to check your work.
6. Use a damp paper towel to wipe away your work. Place the strips, hearts, and marker back in the bag, and return all items to the kit.

Television

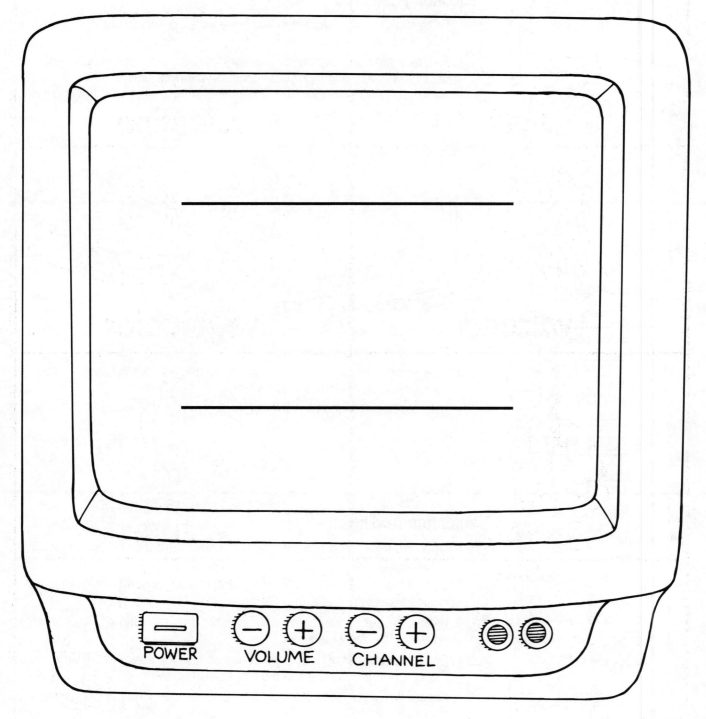

POWER VOLUME CHANNEL

Video of Vocabulary Words

vest

valentine

volcano

vegetables

vet

vulture

vase

van

Valentine Addition

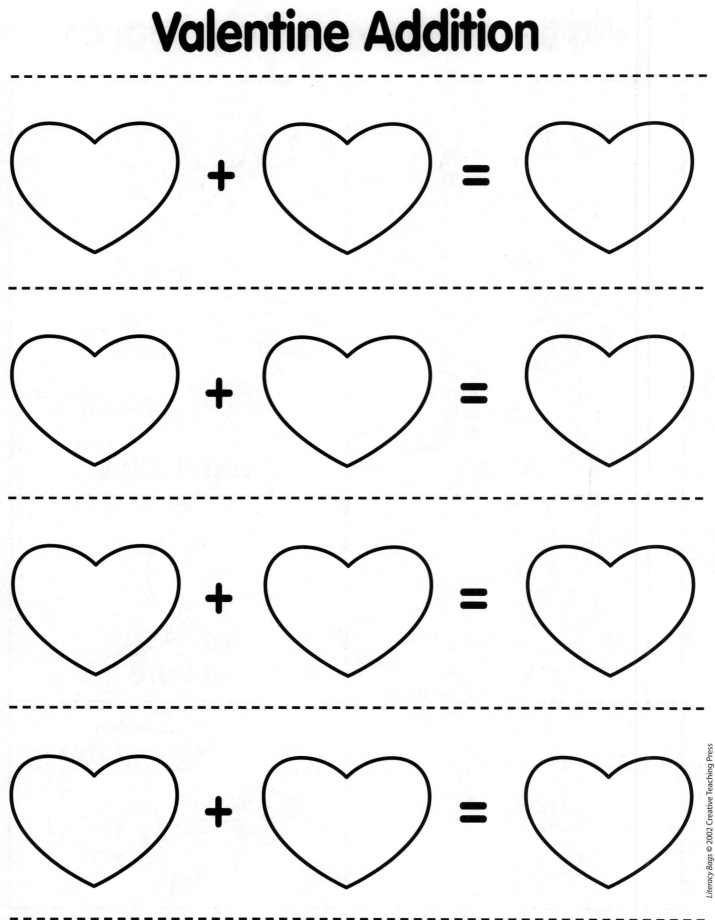

Waterworks

Use a paint marker to write *Waterworks* on one side of a large bucket or pail.

Alternative Theme Ideas

- Find fabric with a wagon, walrus, watch, water, watermelon, weather, whale, wheel, wild west, winter, wizard, world, or worm print, and use it to make a bag (see page 4).

- Tie a whistle to an old-fashioned, metal lunch box, and use a paint marker to write *Whistle While You Work* on one side.

- Find a brightly colored bag, and use a fabric marker to write *Wacky, Wild, and Wonderful Things To Do* on one side.

Literature Links

- ➡ *Baby Beluga* by Raffi (Crown Books)
- ➡ *A Drop of Water: A Book of Science and Wonder* by Walter Wick (Scholastic)
- ➡ *It Looked Like Spilt Milk* by Charles Shaw (HarperCollins)
- ➡ *Kipper's Book of Weather* by Mick Inkpen (Harcourt)
- ➡ *The Magic Schoolbus: At the Waterworks* by Joanna Cole (Scholastic)
- ➡ *Snow White* by Jacob Grimm (Little, Brown and Company)
- ➡ *Whales* by Gail Gibbons (Holiday House)
- ➡ *What's the Weather Like Today?* by Rozanne Lanczak Williams (Creative Teaching Press)
- ➡ *Whistle for Willie* by Ezra Jack Keats (Puffin)
- ➡ *Wombat Divine* by Mem Fox (Harcourt)

Playtime Props

- ★ pinwheels
- ★ walrus, whale, wolf, or worm stuffed animals or puppets
- ★ wands
- ★ washers
- ★ whistles (clean with rubbing alcohol after each use)

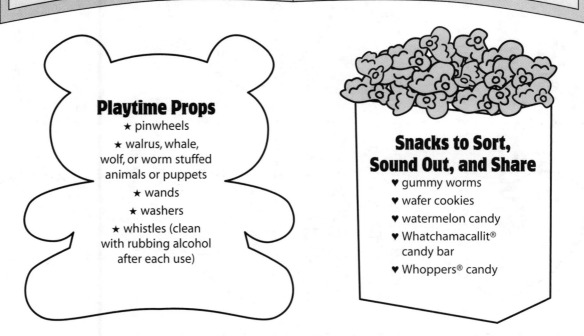

Snacks to Sort, Sound Out, and Share

- ♥ gummy worms
- ♥ wafer cookies
- ♥ watermelon candy
- ♥ Whatchamacallit® candy bar
- ♥ Whoppers® candy

Waterworks
Parent Journal

Please use this journal to record your comments or questions about the games and activities you have enjoyed with your child.

Waterworks
Student Journal

Here are some of the things you can write in this journal.

1. Read one of the books in the kit, and write about your favorite part of the story.

2. Write your own story.

3. Write about some ways that you use water.

4. List as many words as you can that begin with the letter w.

5. Write about your favorite game or activity in this kit. Tell why you liked it.

Remember: Always write your name before you write anything else in the journal!

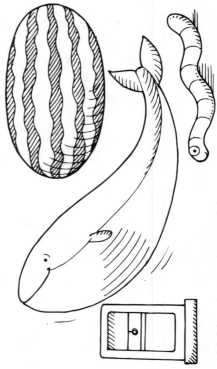

Waterworks Preparations

Weather Watchers

Children will read a pictograph and use it to answer questions.

Copy the **Weather Watchers reproducible (page 155)** for each child, and put the papers in a **file folder**. Glue the **Weather Watchers instruction card (page 154)** to the cover of the folder, and place it in the kit.

Wet Words Ahead

Children will write words with the rime -*et*.

Copy the **Wet Words Ahead reproducible (page 156)**, cut out the clouds, and write _*et* on each cloud. Open a **file folder**, and glue the cloud cutouts to the right side. Write the letters *b, g, l, m, n, p, s,* and *w* across the left side of the folder. Glue the **Wet Words Ahead instruction card (page 154)** to the cover of the folder, and laminate it. Put a **transparency marker** and **cotton balls** in a **resealable bag**. Place the bag and the folder in the kit.

Lightning Words

Children will read words that begin with *w*.

Make two copies of the **Lightning Bolts reproducible (page 157)** on **card stock**, and write each of the following words on a separate lightning bolt: *want, was, we, went, were, what, when, where, which, who, will,* and *with*. Cut out the lightning bolts, and laminate them. Put the lightning bolt cutouts, a **minute timer**, and the **Lightning Words instruction card (page 154)** in a **resealable bag**, and place the bag in the kit.

Waterworks Instruction Cards

Literacy Bags © 2002 Creative Teaching Press

Weather Watchers

Materials
- folder

1. Remove a paper from the folder, and write your name at the top of it.
2. Read the pictograph to see what the weather was like during one week, and then use the pictograph to answer the questions at the bottom of the paper.
3. Place your paper back in the folder, and return the folder to the kit.

Wet Words Ahead

Materials
- folder
- transparency marker
- cotton ball

1. Open the folder, and read the letters on the left side.
2. Use the special marker to write one letter on each cloud to make eight words, and read them aloud.
3. Use a damp cotton ball to wipe the clouds clean.
4. Return all items to the kit.

Lightning Words

Materials
- lightning bolt cutouts
- minute timer

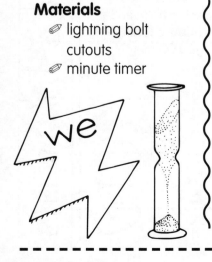

1. Shuffle the cutouts into a pile.
2. Set the timer, and see how many words you can read in a minute.
3. Keep trying until you can read all of the words in a minute.
4. Place the cutouts back in the bag, and return all items to the kit.

Weather Watchers

Sunday 	Monday 	Tuesday 	Wednesday 	Thursday 	Friday 	Saturday 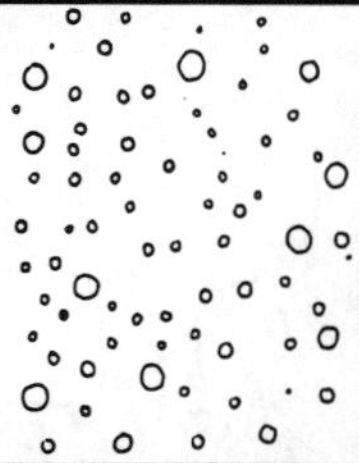

On what day did it rain? _____

On what day did it snow? _____

On what day or days was it cloudy? _____

On what day or days was the sun out? _____

What is your favorite kind of weather? _____

Why do you like this kind of weather? _____

_____

_____

_____

Wet Words Ahead

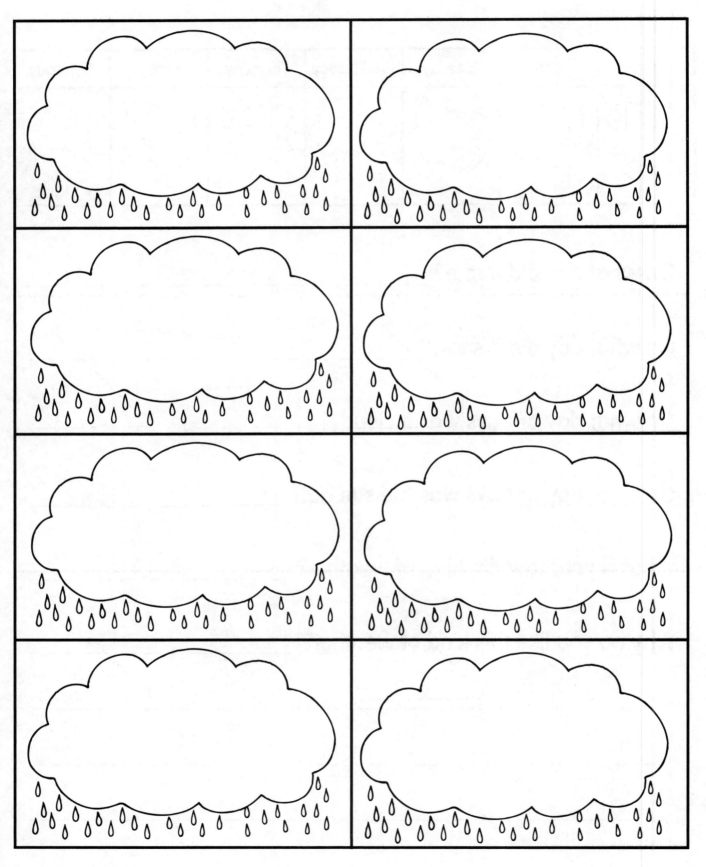

Literacy Bags © 2002 Creative Teaching Press

Lightning Bolts

Our Exciting Box

Cover a box with colorful, patterned contact paper, and use a permanent marker to write *Our Exciting Box* across one side. Cut two slits on the side of the box, put a rope through each slit, and tie a knot on each end to make a handle. Repeat on the opposite side to make another handle.

Alternative Theme Ideas

- Find fabric with an extra-terrestrial, fox, x-ray, or xylophone print, and use it to make a bag (see page 4).

- Find a dinosaur pillowcase or use fabric paint to draw dinosaurs on a plain pillowcase, and use a fabric marker to write *T-Rex and Friends* on it.

Literature Links

- ↬ *Alien & Possum: Friends No Matter What* by Tony Johnston (Simon & Schuster)
- ↬ *Arthur's Chicken Pox* by Marc Brown (Little, Brown and Company)
- ↬ *Fox and His Friends* by Edward Marshall (Puffin Books)
- ↬ *The Fox and the Chicken* by John Archambault and David Plummer (Creative Teaching Press)
- ↬ *Fox in Socks* by Dr. Seuss (Beginner Books)
- ↬ *Hattie and the Fox* by Mem Fox (Aladdin)
- ↬ *Hush, Little Alien* by Daniel Kirk (Hyperion Books)
- ↬ *Itchy, Itchy Chicken Pox* by Grace Maccarone (Scholastic)
- ↬ *Jo Jo in Outer Space* by Margaret Allen (Creative Teaching Press)
- ↬ *The Little Green Man Visits a Farm* by Kimberlee Graves (Creative Teaching Press)

Playtime Props

★ fox or ox
stuffed animal
or puppet

★ xylophone

Snacks to Sort, Sound Out, and Share

♥ Chex® cereal

♥ Extra® gum

♥ Kix® cereal

♥ Trix® cereal

Our Exciting Box
Student Journal

Here are some of the things you can write in this journal.

1. Read one of the books in the kit, and write about your favorite part of the story.

2. Write your own story.

3. What would you put in your own "exciting box"?

4. List as many words as you can that have the letter x in them.

5. Write about your favorite game or activity in this kit. Tell why you liked it.

Remember: Always write your name before you write anything else in the journal!

Our Exciting Box
Parent Journal

Please use this journal to record your comments or questions about the games and activities you have enjoyed with your child.

Our Exciting Box Preparations

Fox in a Box

Children will practice reading and using directional words.

Write on a **sentence strip** *The fox is _____ the box*. Laminate the strip, attach a piece of **Velcro** to the blank line on the strip, and tape the strip to a **shoe box**. Write the following words on separate **index cards**: *inside, outside, above, behind,* and *below*. Laminate the cards, and attach a piece of Velcro to the back of each card. Put the word cards and the **Fox in a Box instruction card (page 161)** in a **resealable bag**. Find a **small fox stuffed animal or puppet**, or cut out a **picture of a fox,** and laminate it, and put it in the bag. Place the bag and the shoe box in the kit.

Extra-Terrestrial Storyboard

Children will tell an original story on a storyboard.

Copy the **Extra-Terrestrial Storyboard reproducible (page 162)** and the **Extra-Terrestrial Characters reproducible (page 163)** on **card stock**, and cut out the characters. Color the characters and the storyboard, and laminate them. Put the character cutouts and the **Extra-Terrestrial Storyboard instruction card (page 161)** in a **resealable bag**. Place the bag and the storyboard in the kit.

Extra Special Tic-Tac-Toe

Children will read words that have the *x* sound in them.

Copy the **Extra Special Tic-Tac-Toe reproducible (page 164)** on **card stock**, and laminate it. Tie a **string** to one end of a **transparency marker**. Hole-punch the top of the reproducible, and tie the other end of the string through it. Put the paper and the **Extra Special Tic-Tac-Toe instruction card (page 161)** in a **resealable bag**, and place the bag in the kit.

Our Exciting Box Instruction Cards

Materials
- Fox in a Box shoe box
- word cards
- fox stuffed animal/puppet or cutout

Fox in a Box

1. Choose a card, and attach it to the sentence strip on the box.
2. Read aloud the sentence, and use the fox and the box to demonstrate what you just read.
3. Remove the card, attach a different one, and demonstrate the new sentence.
4. Repeat the activity with the rest of the cards.
5. Place the cards back in the bag, and return the bag and the shoe box to the kit.

Materials
- Extra-Terrestrial Storyboard
- extra-terrestrial character cutouts
- student journal

Extra-Terrestrial Storyboard

1. Place the storyboard on a flat surface.
2. Arrange the character cutouts on the storyboard.
3. Tell a story about the extra-terrestrial characters. Write your story in the student journal.
4. If you have time, make up another story.
5. Place the character cutouts back in the bag, and return all items to the kit.

Materials
- Extra Special Tic-Tac-Toe board
- transparency marker
- paper towel

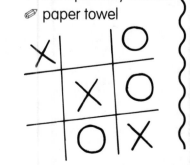

Extra Special Tic-Tac-Toe

1. Ask someone to play this game with you, and decide which person will be x's and which person will be o's.
2. Choose one person to go first. The first player reads a word on the board and uses the special marker to write his or her symbol (x or o) over it.
3. The next player reads another word and uses the special marker to write his or her symbol (x or o) over it.
4. Play continues until one person gets three x's or o's in a row.
5. Use a damp paper towel to wipe the board clean, and play again.
6. Return all items to the kit.

Extra-Terrestrial Storyboard

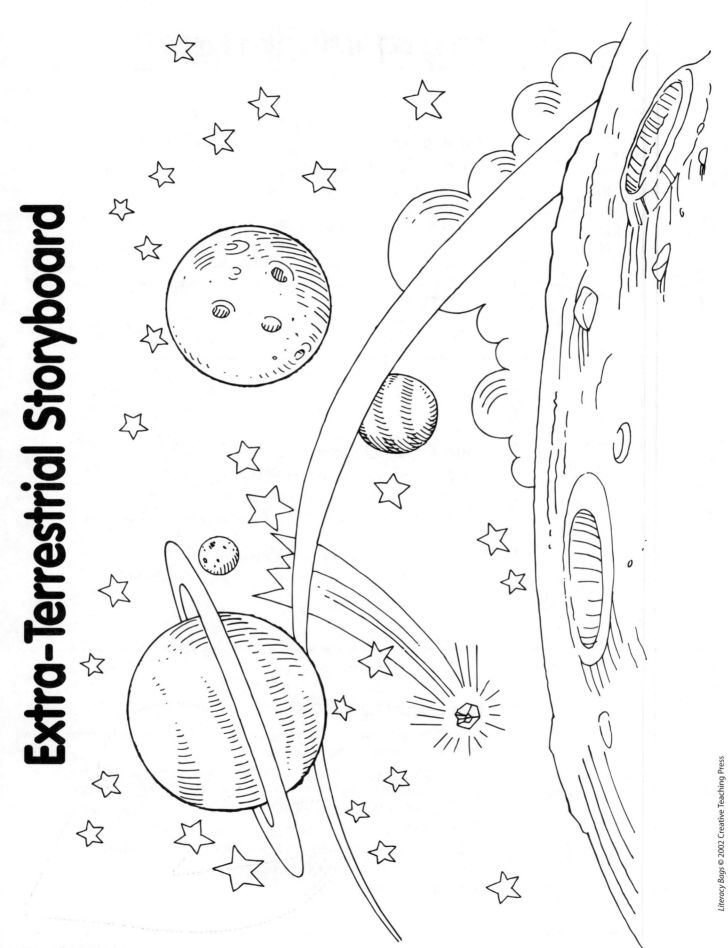

Extra-Terrestrial Characters

Extra Special Tic-Tac-Toe

box	fox	ox
chicken pox	music box	jack-in-the-box
tyrannosaurus rex	X-ray	xylophone

A Year to Remember

Cover a box with yellow contact paper, and paint on each side of the box a separate scene or symbols that represent one of the four seasons. Use a paint marker to write *A Year to Remember* on one side. Cut two slits on the side of the box, insert a rope through each slit, and tie a knot on each end to make a handle. Repeat on the opposite side to make another handle.

Alternative Theme Ideas

- Find fabric with a calendar, yak, yellow flower, or yellow school bus print, and use it to make a bag (see page 4).

- Find a lunch box with a yellow school bus on it.

- Find fabric with a print of children's faces, and use it to make a bag (see page 4). Use a fabric marker to write *Yes, We Can!* on one side.

Literature Links

- *The Bus for Us* by Suzanne Bloom (Boyds Mills Press)
- *A Busy Year* by Leo Lionni (Alfred A. Knopf Books)
- *Cookie's Week* by Cindy Ward (Putnam)
- *From Head to Toe* by Eric Carle (HarperCollins)
- *I Can Do It Myself* by Lessie Little and Eloise Greenfield (Crowell)
- *I'm a Can-Do Kid* by John Archambault and David Plummer (Creative Teaching Press)
- *Jasper's Beanstalk* by Nick Butterworth and Mick Inkpen (Harcourt)
- *No Moon, No Milk!* by Chris Babcock (Crown)
- *Those Can-Do Pigs* by David McPhail (Dutton)
- *A Year for Kiko* by Ferida Wolff (Houghton Mifflin)

Playtime Props

★ toy yellow school bus

★ Yahtzee® Junior game

★ yak or yellow bumblebee stuffed animal or puppet

Snacks to Sort, Sound Out, and Share

♥ lemon cookies

♥ Lemonheads®

A Year to Remember
Parent Journal

Please use this journal to record your comments or questions about the games and activities you have enjoyed with your child.

A Year to Remember
Student Journal

Here are some of the things you can write in this journal.

1. Read one of the books in the kit, and write about your favorite part of the story.

2. Write your own story.

3. Write about your favorite season of the year.

4. List as many words as you can that begin with the letter *y*.

5. Write about your favorite game or activity in this kit. Tell why you liked it.

Remember: Always write your name before you write anything else in the journal!

A Year to Remember Preparations

Yearly Calendar

Children will read a calendar and use it to answer questions.

Copy the **Yearly Calendar reproducible (page 169)** on **card stock**, and laminate it. Laminate a **calendar with all twelve months of the year on one page**. Put the **Yearly Calendar instruction card (page 168)**, the calendar, and a **transparency marker** in a **resealable bag**. Place all items in the kit.

Yes, I Can!

Children will read simple sentences and think about things they can do.

Copy the **Can You Do It? reproducible (page 170)** on **card stock**, laminate it, and cut out the cards. Write *Yes, I Can!* and *No, Not Yet* on separate **index cards**. Put the cards and the **Yes, I Can! instruction card (page 168)** in a **resealable bag**, and place the bag in the kit.

Little Words in Yellow

Children will identify words within words.

Write the words *cat, fall, for, hand, his, little, man, shout,* and *wind* on separate **index cards**, and laminate them. Put the cards, the **Little Words in Yellow instruction card (page 168)**, and a **yellow transparency marker** in a **resealable bag**, and place the bag in the kit.

A Year to Remember Instruction Cards

Materials
- Yearly Calendar paper
- calendar
- transparency marker
- paper towel

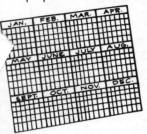

Yearly Calendar

1. Place the Yearly Calendar paper and the calendar side by side on a flat surface.
2. Use the calendar to answer the questions on the paper. Use the special marker to write your answers on the blank lines.
3. Ask someone to check your work.
4. Use a damp paper towel to wipe away your work.
5. Return all items to the kit.

Materials
- Can You Do It? cards
- index cards

Yes, I Can!

1. Place the "Yes, I Can!" card and the "No, Not Yet" card on a flat surface.
2. Read each sentence. If you can do what you just read, place the card below the words "Yes, I Can!" If you cannot yet do what you just read, place the card below the words "No, Not Yet."
3. Place the cards back in the bag, and return the bag to the kit.

Materials
- word cards
- yellow transparency marker
- paper towel

Little Words in Yellow

1. Read each card, look for the "little word" within the "big word," and circle it with the special marker. For example, on the card with the word *his*, circle the word *is*.
2. Ask someone to check your work.
3. Use a damp paper towel to wipe away your work, and place the cards and the marker back in the bag.
4. Return the bag to the kit.

Yearly Calendar

January · February · March · April · May · June · July · August · September · October · November · December

1. How many months are in the year? _____

2. How many months have 31 days? _____
   Circle them on the calendar.

3. Write two months that have 30 days.

   _____ _____

4. Which month comes after April?

   _____

5. Which month comes before February?

   _____

6. In which month do you celebrate your birthday?

   _____

Can You Do It?

I can ride a bike.

I can write my name.

I can tie my shoes.

I can dial my phone number.

I can say my ABCs.

I can say my address.

I can count to 100.

I can read.

Zigzag Bag

Find a plain cloth tote bag, and use fabric paint to decorate it with colorful zigzag designs. Use a fabric marker to write *Zigzag Bag* on one side.

Alternative Theme Ideas

- Find fabric with a zebra, zinnia, zipper, or zoo print, and use it to make a bag (see page 4).

- Use animal-shaped foam sponges to paint zoo animals on a plain pillowcase. Use a fabric marker to write *A Lot to Do at the Zany Zoo* on one side.

- Cover a detergent box with white contact paper, and paint black stripes on it to create a zebra box. Use a paint marker to write *Our Zippy Zebra Box* on one side.

Literature Links

- ➡ *1,2,3 to the Zoo: A Counting Book* by Eric Carle (Philomel)
- ➡ *Fifty Below Zero* by Robert Munsch (Annick Press)
- ➡ *Going to the Zoo* by Tom Paxton (Morrow Junior Books)
- ➡ *Inside a Zoo in the City* by Alyssa Satin Capucilli (Scholastic)
- ➡ *Planting a Rainbow* by Lois Ehlert (Harcourt)
- ➡ *The Z Was Zapped* by Chris Van Allsburg (Houghton Mifflin)
- ➡ *Zigzag: The Sound of Z* by Alice K. Flanagan (Child's World)
- ➡ *Zin! Zin! Zin! A Violin* by Lloyd Moss (Simon & Schuster)
- ➡ *Zoo Looking* by Mem Fox (Mondo)
- ➡ *Zoom! Zoom! Zoom! I'm Off to the Moon* by Dan Yaccarino (Scholastic)

Playtime Props
- ★ zebra stuffed animal or puppet
- ★ zoo rummy

Snacks to Sort, Sound Out, and Share
- ♥ Fudge Shoppe® Fudge Stripes cookies
- ♥ Little Debbie® Zebra Cakes
- ♥ Zesta® crackers
- ♥ Zingers®

Zigzag Bag
Parent Journal

Please use this journal to record your comments or questions about the games and activities you have enjoyed with your child.

Zigzag Bag
Student Journal

Here are some of the things you can write in this journal.

1. Read one of the books in the kit, and write about your favorite part of the story.

2. Write your own story.

3. Draw a zigzag design.

4. List as many words as you can that begin with the letter z.

5. Write about your favorite game or activity in this kit. Tell why you liked it.

Remember: Always write your name before you write anything else in the journal!

Zigzag Bag Preparations

Zigzagging Zoo Animals

Children will identify words that begin with z.

Copy the **Zigzagging Zoo Animals reproducible (page 175)** on **card stock**, and laminate it. Place the paper, a **transparency marker**, and the **Zigzagging Zoo Animals instruction card (page 174)** in a **resealable bag**. Place the bag in the kit.

Zinnias

Children will observe a seed sprout.

Put **zinnia seeds** in a **small resealable bag** and **potting soil** and **peat moss** in separate **large resealable bags**. Put **plastic cups** and the **Zinnias instruction card (page 174)** in a separate resealable bag. Place all the bags in the kit.

Zero the Hero

Children will place multiples of ten in ascending order.

Make ten copies of the **Zero the Hero reproducible (page 176)** on **card stock**. Use **glitter pens** to write each multiple of 10 from 10 to 100 on a separate Zero the Hero figure, cut out the figures, and laminate them. Put the Zero the Hero cutouts and the **Zero the Hero instruction card (page 174)** in a **resealable bag**, and place the bag in the kit.

Zigzag Bag Instruction Cards

Materials
- Zigzagging Zoo Animals paper
- transparency marker
- paper towel

Zigzagging Zoo Animals

1. Place the Zigzagging Zoo Animals paper on a flat surface.
2. Ask someone to read the story with you.
3. Use the special marker to draw a zigzag line under each word that has z in it.
4. Draw a circle around the name of each zoo animal.
5. Answer the questions at the bottom of the paper.
6. Use a damp paper towel to wipe away your work, and return all items to the kit.

Materials
- cups
- potting soil
- peat moss
- zinnia seeds

Zinnias

1. Place a cup on a flat surface, and fill it with a little potting soil and a little peat moss.
2. Place a few zinnia seeds in the cup, and cover them with some more soil and peat moss.
3. Add ¼ cup water to the soil, and place the cup by a sunny window.
4. Watch for the seeds to sprout, and water the soil when it gets too dry.
5. Return all items (except your plant) to the kit.

Materials
- Zero the Hero cutouts

Zero the Hero

1. Place the cutouts faceup on a flat surface, and read the numbers on them.
2. Place the cutouts in order from smallest to largest, and read the numbers again.
3. Place the cutouts back in the bag, and return it to the kit.

Zigzagging Zoo Animals

Zachary went to the Zippity Zoo. He zigzagged from cage to cage watching the zany animals zip here and there. At the lion's den, the lion roared so loudly that Zachary quickly zoomed away. At the elephant's pen, the mother elephant was washing her calf's fuzzy hair. Then she stopped to eat some zucchini and other vegetables. Zachary went to see the monkeys next. They zigged and zagged from tree to tree. Zachary's next stop was to see Zoro the rhinoceros who was lying in the mud. At last, Zachary went to see his favorite animal, the zebra. And what a zealous zebra it was! Zachary soon became tired from visiting all of those zany animals, so he went home to catch some zzzz's.

How many words with z did you circle? _____

How many zoo animals are in the story? _____

Zero the Hero

Literacy Bags © 2002 Creative Teaching Press